How Are We Governed in the '80s?

How Are We Governed in the '80s?

John Ricker
and
John Saywell
with Alan Skeoch

Clarke, Irwin & Company Limited
Toronto/Vancouver

ISBN 0-7720-1418-3

Canadian Cataloguing in Publication Data
   Ricker, John, 1923-
     How are we governed in the '80s?

   Previous ed. by J. Ricker and J. Saywell.
   Includes index.
   ISBN 0-7720-1418-3

   1. Canada — Politics and government. I. Saywell, John
   1929-   II. Skeoch, Alan. III. Title.

   JL65   1966.R48   1982   320.971   C82-094954-X

ACKNOWLEDGEMENTS

The authors and publisher wish to thank Historical Services and Consultants Ltd. for researching the illustrative materials and the following individuals and organizations for permission to include the illustrations listed. The publisher welcomes any information which will enable him, in subsequent printings, to correct any errors made in giving credit lines.

Archives of Ontario, 13 (middle right), 42 (top, bottom right). Archives of Saskatchewan, 64 (top). Josh Beutel, *Saint John Telegraph-Journal*, 97 (as appeared in the report of *The Royal Commission On Newspapers*). CANAPRESS Photo Service (Canadian Press Photographs), 16, 27 (bottom left), 32 (top), 52 (top right, middle, and bottom left), 64 (middle two, bottom right), 66, 67 (bottom middle and right), 71, 73 (bottom three), 79 (all), 80, 89 (bottom), 131, 134 (middle right), 135 (bottom three), 138, 165 (top). CBC Photo, 113 (photo Fred Phipps, left). Robert Chambers, *The Halifax Chronicle-Herald*, 29, 40, 85 (bottom), 136. City of Toronto, 157. City of Toronto Archives, 22, 122 (bottom), 163. John Collins, *The Montreal Gazette*, 57, 101 (right), 139. *Community Ontario*, Vol. 26, Number 2, 145 (bottom). CPR, 24 (bottom left). CTV Photo, 113 (middle). Julie Dale for the Arch Dale cartoons, 60 (left), 102 (both). Department of Ambulance Services, The Municipality of Metropolitan Toronto, 153 (middle). *The Financial Post*, 33 (Christopher Waddell). Bryce Flynn, 27 (bottom second from left). Franklin in *The Globe and Mail*, Toronto, 68. General Motors of Canada, 27 (bottom right). Glenbow Foundation, 24 (top), 122 (top). Global TV Photo, 113 (right). *The Globe and Mail*, Toronto, 48 (top left), 49 (bottom). Grain Growers' Guide, February 26, 1913, 42 (photo from The McClung Papers, top). Imperial Oil Limited, 27 (top two left). Peter Ittinuar, 52 (middle right). Anthony Jenkins, *The Globe and Mail*, Toronto, 81, 102 (as appeared in the report of *The Royal Commission On Newspapers*). Yardley Jones, *The Montreal Star*, 35. Flora MacDonald, 51. Manitoba Archives, 24 (bottom right). Pauline McGibbon, 148. McNally, *The Montreal Star*, 132. Miller Services, 167. New Brunswick Museum, 25 (bottom right). NFB Photothèque, ONF, 27 (photo Dr. Andrew Farquar, top left, middle right), 49 (photo Bob Anderson, top right), 76 (photo Bob Anderson). Len Norris and *The Vancouver Sun*, 85 (top). Nova Scotia Information Service, 27 (top right). Ontario Ministry of Industry and Tourism, 73 (top), 145 (top left). Ontario Ministry of Municipal Affairs and Housing, 10, 153 (top left, middle left and right, bottom right), 161. Ottawa City Hall, 145 (top right). Roy Peterson, 108 (as appeared in the report of *The Royal Commission On Newspapers*). Provincial Archives, Victoria, B.C., 24 (middle left), 60 (left). Public Archives Canada, 13 (top, middle right, both bottom), 25 (top three right, middle left, bottom left), 39 (Macpherson), 67 (top three, middle right), 83 (Macpherson), 87 (Macpherson), 89 (top two), 117 (Macpherson, both), 127 (Macpherson). RCMP, 24 (top middle). Rusins and *The Ottawa Citizen*, 134 (middle left). Jeanne Sauvé, 52 (photo Gaby, top left). Simcoe South, Voters' List, 48 (top right). Spadina Riding, 1981 By-election, 49 (top left). The Toronto *Star* Syndicate, 31 (Macpherson), 32 (bottom), 48 (top left, bottom), 63 (Macpherson), 64 (bottom left), 67 (bottom left), 135 (top). Toronto Stock Exchange, 27 (bottom second from right). Toronto Transit Commission, 153 (bottom left). E. D. Uluschak, *The Edmonton Journal*, 9, 91, 101 (left), 110, 140. United Auto Workers, *Solidarity Canada*, 101 (Carless, top). Vancouver Public Library, 24 (bottom left). *The Vancouver Sun*, 158.

Contents

Acknowledgements / 4
Introduction / 7

Chapter 1: How Are We Governed? / 8
What Do We Mean by Government? / 11
What Kind of Government Has Canada? / 12
What Is Canada's Constitution? / 14
Study Guide / 18

Chapter 2: What Is Our Political System? / 20
How Does Our Environment Shape the
   Political System? / 23
How Do Our Demands Reach Government? / 30
How Do Governments Respond? / 34
Study Guide / 36

Chapter 3: How Does Democracy Work? / 38
Who Can Vote? / 41
Are All Votes Equal? / 43
Does the Majority Rule? / 45
How Are Elections Held? / 47
Who Can Run? Who Does Run? / 50
Study Guide / 54

Chapter 4: Why Political Parties? / 56
What Does a Political Party Stand For? / 58
How Are Political Parties Organized? / 62
How Important Is the Party Leader? / 65
Study Guide / 70

**Chapter 5: How Does Parliamentary
Government Work? / 72**
Who Makes the Laws in Canada? / 75
Why Is the Cabinet So Powerful? / 81
What Does the Cabinet Do? / 84
Do We Need a Senate? / 85
Do We Need a Governor General? / 88
Are We Governed by the Civil Service? / 91
Study Guide / 94

Chapter 6: Should We Rely on the Mass Media? / 96
How Healthy Is Our Press? / 98
Who Owns the Press? / 102
Do Advertisers Influence the Press? / 108
How Has the Government Responded? / 110
The Canadian Broadcasting Corporation:
    How Well Does It Perform? / 111
Study Guide / 114

Chapter 7: Canadian Federalism:
How Does It Work? / 116
Why Does Canada Have a Federal System? / 118
Why Has Canada's Federal System Changed? / 120
How Can We Change Our Federal System? / 129
Quebec: Why Is It Different? / 130
Study Guide / 142

Chapter 8: Provincial and Local Governments:
What Role Do They Play? / 144
Are Provincial Governments Different? / 146
What Do the Provincial Governments Do? / 149
Why Have Local Government? / 151
How Are Local Governments Organized? / 154
Local Government: The Cradle of Democracy? / 160
Study Guide / 162

Chapter 9: What Is the Rule of Law? / 164
What Is the Rule of Law? / 166
How Does The Canada Act, 1982,
    Protect Our Freedom? / 168
Canadian Charter of Rights and Freedoms / 169
The Judiciary / 184
Study Guide / 188

Index 190

Introduction

This book provides a beginning for anyone who wishes to answer the question, *How Are We Governed in the '80s?* It is only a beginning, for each chapter could be a book in itself. Library shelves are filled with books on democracy, parliamentary government, the Cabinet, political parties, the role of the prime minister, the press, federalism, and law. However, there are still a great many questions to be answered, and in each chapter, we raise as many questions as we answer.

Does our democratic system enable the will of the people to become the policy of the government? Do our political parties think of our interests first and their hold on power second? What kind of federal system will keep Canada united and prosperous? Should the provinces be given more power? Should Quebec be accepted as a province different from others? Closer to home, why do so few of us take an interest in local government?

We wrote the first edition of *How Are We Governed?* more than twenty years ago, and every few years we brought it up to date. But finally we decided to write a new book, for Canada had changed a great deal in twenty years.

How Are We Governed in the '80s? is, in some ways, similar to the old. After all, the working of parliamentary government, the role of political parties, the nature of democracy, the importance of the press, and the troublesome and difficult issues that face our federal system have not disappeared — nor will they.

Yet this book is also very different. It places government within the broader framework of our political system — the historical, economic, and social environments within which governments must work. It takes a new approach to the problems facing the Canadian federal system. We have included the text of the new *Charter of Rights and Freedoms*, which will be so important in the years to come, and have offered our comments on it. There are many photographs, cartoons, and diagrams to enrich the text.

In principle, however, *How Are We Governed in the '80s?* bears the stamp of its ancestor. Like its predecessor, this new book is based on our continuing conviction that effective citizenship depends upon a real understanding of the way our governments work. Now, as seldom before in our history, there is an urgent need to understand the Canadian political system. We think *How Are We Governed in the '80s?* provides a sound introduction to that study and the basis for an intelligent discussion of current Canadian issues.

Chapter 1
HOW ARE
WE GOVERNED?

What Do We Mean by Government?
Functions of Government

What Kind of Government Has Canada?
Democracy
Monarchy
Parliamentary Government
Cabinet Government
Federal Government

What Is Canada's Constitution?
The Written Constitution
The Unwritten Constitution

"I haven't given the constitution much thought — we've been too busy trying to decide whether to go cold or hungry this winter."

How are we governed? To many Canadians of all ages, this question is not immediately exciting. Most might agree that the question should be looked into — some other time. Right now there are more important matters. If it is winter, some Canadians will be wondering if the snowplows have cleared the roads so that they can reach the skating rink. Others will be concerned that the snowplows may have blocked their driveways and that they will be late for work or school. If summer is near, students may be looking for summer jobs. Regardless of the season, their parents may be worrying about the chances of layoffs at the factory or office.

None of these matters of everyday concern seems directly related to the question, "How are we governed?" Yet they are. Governments cannot control the amount of snow that falls. But they do decide how many snowplows to use and which roads to plow first. Governments cannot guarantee that all students and their parents will have work. Yet governments play a large part in building a healthy economy in which most of us can find work.

In fact, no matter what we talk about, it is hard to avoid the topic of government. When we complain about taxes, protest the pollution that kills our lakes and rivers, or criticize the actions of the Russians or Americans, we are also talking about government. In modern society, government is everywhere. Governments record our births, marriages and deaths. Governments know, or at least try to know, how much money we make. They decide how much of it they will take and what they will do with it. Every time we turn on a light or a tap, get into a car, shop at the supermarket, go to school, attend a

One of the many activities of government that may determine whether we go cold or hungry this winter.

movie, call a doctor or go to a hospital, use the telephone or turn on the television, build an addition to the house or rent an apartment, we are closely controlled by governments.

If they were asked the question directly, "How are we governed?", many Canadians might reply, "Not very well." Most of us can point to features of our society that we think should be changed or improved. In a way, we look on governments as we do on football coaches. If they are winning, that is what they are supposed to do. But there is no reason that they should not do better. If they are losing, we should replace them. But neither countries nor football teams are easy to run. There are no simple ways to ensure a "winning season" in politics or football. If we are to be more than weekend armchair critics, we have to try to gain a real understanding of the nature of the "game."

WHAT DO WE MEAN BY GOVERNMENT?

This is the most basic question in a study of government. A simple definition would be: the organization of society for common action. What does this mean? There are many things that individuals acting on their own cannot do very well, if at all. No one person can act as a police force or army in the face of criminals or invaders. No one person can build or maintain the roads and schools or provide the many services that are required in a modern state. A government is the machinery that individuals set up to enable them to do with others what they cannot do on their own. Without some form of government to provide order, individuals would not be able to protect their property or their lives. The most basic task of government is to make a set of rules that allow the individual members of a society to live together in peace and security. Government must also make sure that the rules are obeyed. It must set up penalties that will protect the interests of the group as a whole against the greed or ambition of any one person or any one group.

There are many different kinds of governments. But they all carry out three main tasks or functions: legislative, executive and judicial. The *legislative* function is concerned with making laws or passing legislation. The *executive* involves putting the laws into effect on a day-to-day basis. The *judicial* function is to decide whether an individual has broken society's laws and to punish the guilty.

Functions of Government

WHAT KIND OF GOVERNMENT HAS CANADA?

There are at least five answers to this question. Some would say that Canada is a democracy, or a monarchy. Others would say that we have a parliamentary system, or cabinet government, or a federal system. The rest of this book explains why each of these answers is correct and why each must be understood in order to answer the big question, "How *are* we governed?" At this stage, we need to have only a general understanding of the terms and why it is proper to use them to describe the government of Canada.

Democracy

Those who say Canada is a democracy are thinking about the way we choose our government or rulers. The word democracy comes from the Greek *demokratia*. This is a combination of two Greek words: *demos*, people, and *kratos*, power. In other words, democracy is a system of government in which the people have power or the people rule. It is not possible today for all of the people in any country to govern. Thus in modern states, democracy means a system in which the citizens of a country freely choose the people who will govern them. In a democracy like Canada, this means that we elect others to represent us in governing the country. For this reason, we sometimes describe our system as *representative government*.

Monarchy

It is also correct to say that Canada is a monarchy. The head of the government of Canada is a monarch, the Queen of Canada. In theory, the monarch is the source of all authority. In Canada, the monarch is represented by the Governor General. But neither the Queen nor the Governor General plays a major role in the actual government of the country. People who say Canada is a monarchy are thinking about the form or outward appearance of Canadian government rather than the way it works in practice. If you knew only that Canada was a monarchy you would not understand the true nature of our government.

Parliamentary Government

Those who say that Canada has a parliamentary government are also right. Parliament in Canada consists of the Queen, represented by the Governor General, the Senate, whose members are appointed, and the House of Commons, made up of representatives elected by the Canadian voters. Parliamentary government in Canada means government by Queen, Senate, and House of Commons.

The Battle of St. Eustache, 1837

Responsible government had to be won in both Canada and England. Although the British had responsible government by the 1830s, the British government did not think it was possible for a colony to have the same system. If the Governor, like the monarch, had to act on the advice of his ministers, how could he also be responsible to the Mother Country for the government of the colony? But as time passed, British North Americans grew determined to have a more democratic system. Finally, they demanded responsible government. These men and these events chart the course of the struggle that finally won responsible government for the colonies.

William Lyon Mackenzie

Lord Durham

Joseph Howe

Burning of the Parliament Buildings, 1849

Parliamentary government is based on the British parliamentary system. Parliament began in England. For many years it was dominated by the monarchs. They were the real rulers of the kingdom and they looked on Parliament as their servant. Over many years, the power of the monarch declined and Parliament became the ruler of England. Within Parliament, the House of Commons, made up of the elected representatives of the people, became the most important and powerful part of the government. The monarch's ministers in the Cabinet, who did the actual work of running the country, came to be responsible to the House of Commons rather than to the King or Queen.

Cabinet Government

In many ways the Cabinet is the heart of our parliamentary system of government. It is because of its great power that many Canadians refer to our system as cabinet government. The cabinet ministers carry out the executive functions of government. They must be elected to the House of Commons or have seats in the Senate. To stay in office, they must have the support of a majority of the members of the House of Commons. In other words, the cabinet ministers, the executive branch of government, are responsible to the House of Commons, the legislative branch. The House of Commons, in turn, is elected by, and responsible to, the people. Therefore, a line of responsibility runs from the bottom to the top of our system of government. Because of this responsibility, Canadians sometimes use the term *responsible government* to describe our system.

Federal Government

What do people mean when they say that Canada has a federal system of government? They mean that Canada has a system in which the power to make laws is shared between two levels of government — a national or central government and the provincial governments. Because both levels of government have the power to make laws, Canada is a federation, or has a federal system of government.

WHAT IS CANADA'S CONSTITUTION?

In the later 1970s and early 1980s, Canadians heard a great deal about their *constitution*. What does the word mean? When we are talking about government, the word constitution means the basic principles, laws, and rules under which the country is governed. Constitutions usually say what the

CANADA'S WRITTEN CONSTITUTION

THE CANADA ACT, 1982

includes

1. The Constitution Act, 1867 (British North America Act, 1867)

2. The acts bringing British Columbia, Manitoba, Prince Edward Island, Alberta, Saskatchewan, and Newfoundland into Confederation

3. The Statute of Westminster, 1931

4. All amendments to The British North America Act, 1867

5. The Constitution Act, 1982

powers and duties of the government are and what the rights of the people are. In answering the question, "How are we governed?", we might also have said that we have *constitutional government*. In some ways, that general answer would have been best. For it draws attention to the most important fact of our system of democratic government. It operates in accordance with the basic law of the land or the constitution.

Some constitutions, like that of the United States, are almost completely "written." This means that the principles and laws by which the American government functions are set down in one document. By contrast, the constitution of Great Britain is to a large extent "unwritten." There is no one document to which we can turn to find the basic principles of the British system. The constitution of Canada is both written and unwritten.

The Written Constitution

The "written" part of Canada's constitution is the Canada Act, 1982. On April 17, 1982, in Ottawa, Canada's Queen, Elizabeth II, signed this historic act into law. One section of this act, the Constitution Act, 1982, provides a written *Charter of Rights and Freedoms* that sets out for the first time the legal

Queen Elizabeth II of Canada gives Royal Assent to the Canada Act in Ottawa, April 17, 1982, as Prime Minister Trudeau and members of the federal Cabinet look on.

and democratic rights of Canadians. The Canada Act also "patriated" or brought home from Great Britain a number of other important acts. These acts had been passed in Great Britain on our behalf and had been a part of our constitution. The most important of them was the British North America Act of 1867. This act created the Dominion of Canada and set up our federal and parliamentary system of government. In Canada's new constitution, the British North America Act was renamed the *Constitution Act, 1867*. The new *Charter of Rights and Freedoms* and the federal system of government are part of Canada's written constitution.

The British North America Act of 1867 also said that Canada would have a "Constitution similar in principle to that of the United Kingdom." These few words are very important. They meant that Canada would have a government in which the Cabinet was responsible to the House of Commons. To a large extent, this system of responsible government is part of Canada's "unwritten" constitution. No one document created responsible government, or describes how it will work. Responsible government depends for its existence and its functioning on unwritten rules and practices that have developed over hundreds of years of British and Canadian history.

The Unwritten Constitution

When we speak of the Canadian constitution, we mean the whole system of government in Canada. This includes parliamentary and cabinet government, the federal system, the rule of law and democracy. We will look at all of these more fully in the rest of the book.

STUDY GUIDE

The Study Guide at the end of each chapter serves three purposes. "Getting the Facts" enables the reader to review the essential material in each chapter. The social sciences include the study of government and politics. In some important ways, the social sciences are similar to the natural sciences. Both use words and concepts that must be learned; otherwise there can be no understanding. Physics cannot be understood unless we know about atoms and molecules, mass and energy. Government cannot be understood unless we know the meaning of democracy and law, Parliament and federalism. The first part in "Getting the Facts" in each chapter lists words and concepts that need to be understood.

Second, "Using the Facts" enables the reader to apply the knowledge gained from the chapter in different ways and situations.

Third, the "Research Projects" section encourages the reader to acquire more information in order to provide a deeper and richer understanding of Canadian government and politics. The projects may be pursued individually or as class projects which can stimulate discussion and debate. The research itself will help to develop other important skills: the ability to ask questions, locate and select source materials, and to present conclusions in an organized manner.

Most school and public libraries will have a number of books on Canadian government and politics that can be used for further study and research projects. The *Encyclopedia Canadiana* is always a useful reference work. *The Government of Canada*, by R. MacGregor Dawson and revised by Norman Ward, is perhaps the best over-all text on Canadian government. *The Canadian Political System* by Richard Van Loon and M. S. Whittington is the best book using the "systems" approach that we discuss in Chapter 2. For current developments consult *The Canadian Annual Review of Public Affairs* edited by John Saywell from 1960 to 1978 and by R. B. Byers since 1979.

Getting the Facts

1. Define the following words: government, law, authority, responsible, federal, provincial, appointed, elected, role, rule, power, citizen, nation, country, Parliament, society, constitution.

2. "There are many different kinds of government. But they all carry out three main tasks or functions: legislative, executive and judicial." In your own words, explain what is meant by each function. Give an example of each function. Use a club or organization with which you are familiar as the basis for your answer.

3. What is meant by each of the following terms when they are used to describe the government of Canada: democratic, monarchical, parliamentary, cabinet, and federal?

1. "Without some form of government to provide order, individuals would not be able to protect their property or their lives." Not everyone agrees with this statement in the text. Some great thinkers have argued that government is not necessary. They suggest that it restricts freedom so much that it would be better if there were no government. Draw up a table with two columns headed:

Government Necessary	Government Unnecessary

Under each heading, list as many arguments as you can to support each statement. What is your own conclusion? Why?

2. "In modern society, government is everywhere."
   (a) Give ten examples of how government affects the daily lives of Canadians.
   (b) Try to list ten things you did today that had nothing to do with government.
   (c) Can government affect the way you think? Give examples to support your answer.

3. Write a short, imaginary account of how and why the first government may have been established on earth.

4. Look again at the cartoon on the opening page of this chapter. What point is the cartoonist trying to make? Has he missed the point made in this chapter?

1. Prepare short reports on the importance of the men and events shown on page 13 to the achievement of responsible government.

2. Read one daily newspaper and watch one television news program and list the occasions where "the government" is mentioned. How many different aspects of our lives are included? How many different governments are mentioned? What conclusions can you draw from this project?

Chapter 2
WHAT IS OUR POLITICAL SYSTEM?

How Does Our Environment Shape the Political System?
Geography
History
Society
Economy
Values and Beliefs
Demands for Action

How Do Our Demands Reach Government?
Mass Media
Pressure Groups
Political Parties
Elections

How Do Governments Respond?
Policies and Regulations
Laws

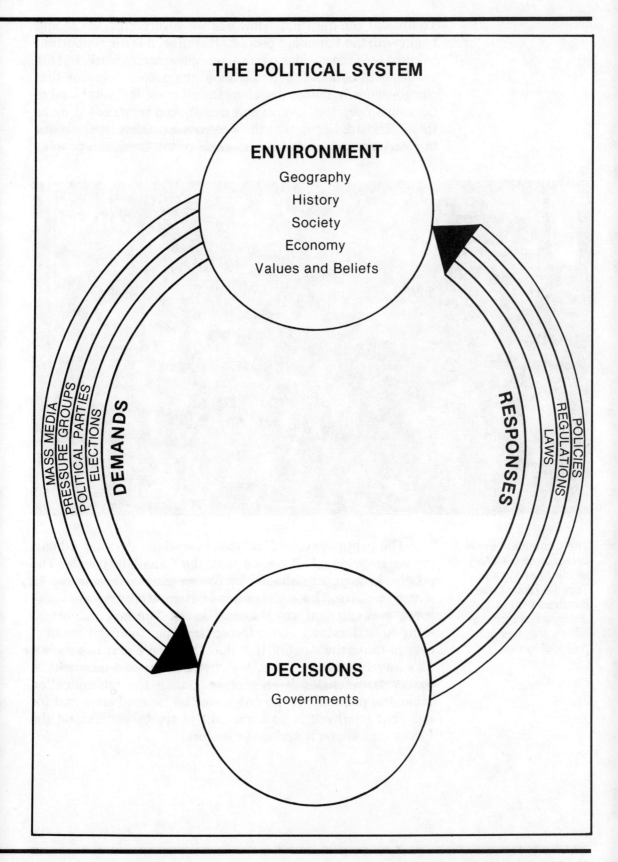

THE POLITICAL SYSTEM

ENVIRONMENT

Geography

History

Society

Economy

Values and Beliefs

DEMANDS

MASS MEDIA
PRESSURE GROUPS
POLITICAL PARTIES
ELECTIONS

RESPONSES

POLICIES
REGULATIONS
LAWS

DECISIONS

Governments

To answer the question "How *are* we governed?", we should begin with the Canadian people. Of course, it is also important to know how the various parts of our government work. But the government cannot function without the people. It is true that our government makes decisions for all of us. But what kind of decisions does the government make? And why does it make them? The answer is that the government makes its decisions in response to the wishes and needs of the Canadian people.

The Canadian people celebrating a victory in the Boer War in Toronto almost one hundred years ago. As they have changed, so, too, has our political system.

The political system includes everything that has a bearing on government. It begins with the Canadian people. The people, in turn, are shaped by forces in the environment in which they live. These forces are of many kinds. Physical, cultural, and spiritual are the most basic. The most important thing to understand about the environment and the political system that grows out of it is that they are always changing. Like any system in nature, the environment and the political system are constantly in motion. Unlike the multiplication table, the political system can never be learned once and for all. That is why it is so important to try to understand the forces that shape it and make it work.

HOW DOES OUR ENVIRONMENT
SHAPE THE POLITICAL SYSTEM?

The political system begins with the environment within which the people live. Here exist the most basic factors that affect all our lives. Sooner or later, these factors lead us to demand decisions from our government. The factors are the same in any political system. Their effects, however, vary greatly from country to country and even from region to region within the same country.

What are these environmental factors? At the most basic level, they include geography and history. They include as well the type of people who live in the country, or society. Of great importance also is the way we produce and exchange goods and services, or the economy. These factors make up our political environment. As individuals, we cannot escape them, although we are not always aware of their influence on the way we think or the way our government functions. As these factors interact, they produce the energy that becomes the life force of our political system.

Canada is a vast country, the second largest in the world. Internally, geography has determined that Canadians will be spread out over a number of very different regions. Frequently they are cut off from easy communication with one another. Often the interests of the people in the various regions are not just different, but in conflict.

Geography

Geography has also determined that modern Canada cannot live cut off from the rest of the world. It must play a part on the world stage whether its people want to or not. Canada is a North Atlantic country with close links with the countries of western Europe. It is a North American country. Separated by a line on a map that marks thousands of kilometres of almost unguarded borders, it is closely tied in every way to the United States. It is a Pacific country. Today it is increasingly influenced by events in Japan, China and the countries of Southeast Asia. It is also an Arctic country whose northern neighbours are the Soviet Union, Greenland, Iceland and the Scandinavian countries.

In many respects, Canada was created in spite of geography. History explains why Canada became and is a nation. It also helps to explain some of the political upheavals that have made the country hard to govern. As might be expected, people in the different regions of the country have different

History

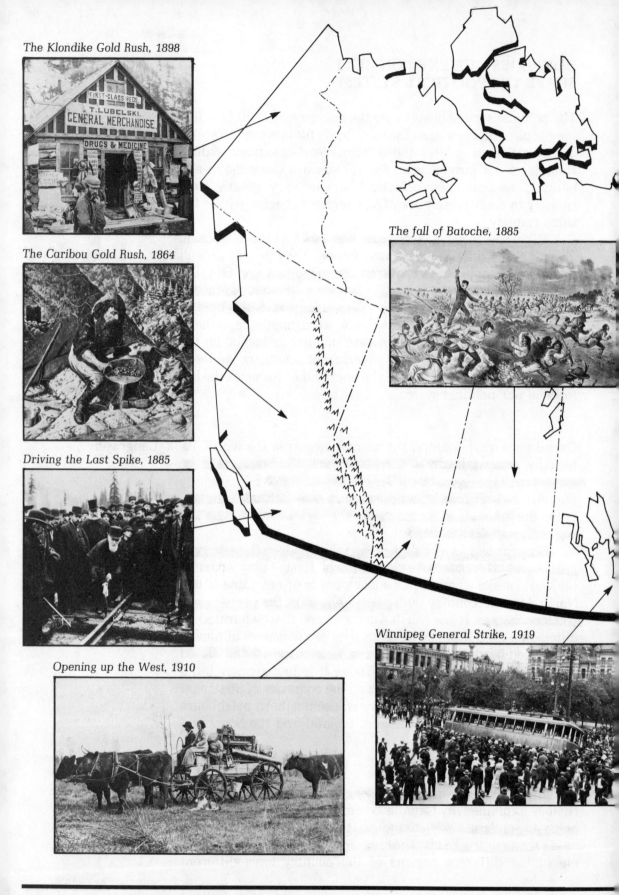

The Klondike Gold Rush, 1898

The Caribou Gold Rush, 1864

Driving the Last Spike, 1885

Opening up the West, 1910

The fall of Batoche, 1885

Winnipeg General Strike, 1919

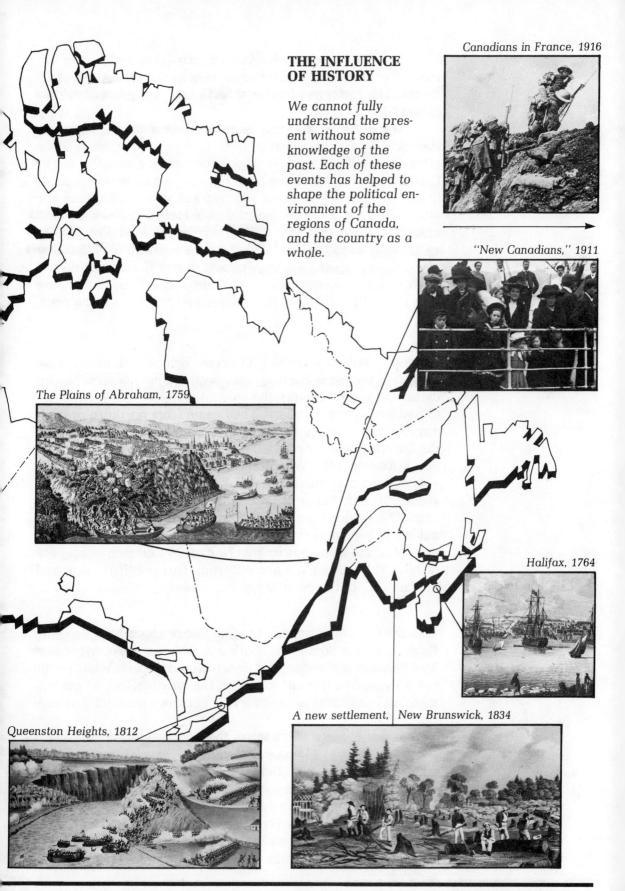

THE INFLUENCE OF HISTORY

We cannot fully understand the present without some knowledge of the past. Each of these events has helped to shape the political environment of the regions of Canada, and the country as a whole.

Canadians in France, 1916

"New Canadians," 1911

The Plains of Abraham, 1759

Halifax, 1764

Queenston Heights, 1812

A new settlement, New Brunswick, 1834

histories. The history of the Atlantic provinces and British Columbia, of Ontario and the Prairie provinces are strikingly different. The history of Quebec is different from that of all the others.

Past experiences also shape the views of newcomers to Canada. Recent immigrants from Europe or Africa or Asia often have different ideas about the country and the world than Canadians who have lived here for many years. Regardless of origins, the views of younger and older Canadians are often different. To some Canadians, history stresses the value of keeping close ties with the United States. To others, history underlines the threat the United States poses to the existence of an independent Canadian nation. Since Canadians do not always share a common view of their past, it is not surprising that they often disagree on policies and actions for the present.

Society

Just as Canada is a land of different regions and histories, so Canadian society is made up of many different peoples. The Indians and the Inuit were the only native Canadians. All other Canadians are newcomers. They came from northern or eastern Europe, from the Mediterranean lands, from countries on the Indian Ocean or along the Pacific Rim, from Africa, from South America, the West Indies, and the United States. Probably every major religion in the world has its churches or synagogues, its temples or prayer halls somewhere in Canada. We cannot walk along the streets of any major Canadian city without being aware of the diversity of the Canadian people. We are not of the same age or sex. Nor are we all rich or all poor or all middle class. We are different. Our political ideas and actions reflect the diversity of our society.

Economy

Like the Canadian people, the Canadian economy is also very diverse. This is another way of saying that we make our livings in a great many ways. And as we would expect, what we do for a living has a great effect on the way we look at government and the kinds of policies and actions we demand or support.

In some parts of Canada, the economy is based almost wholly on the use of natural resources: farms, forests, mines, fisheries, oil and gas fields. Canadians who work at jobs related to natural resources depend to a large extent on trade with other countries for their livelihood, for Canada produces more goods from natural resources than can be sold within the country. Canadians involved with natural resources want governments to do everything they can to promote foreign trade.

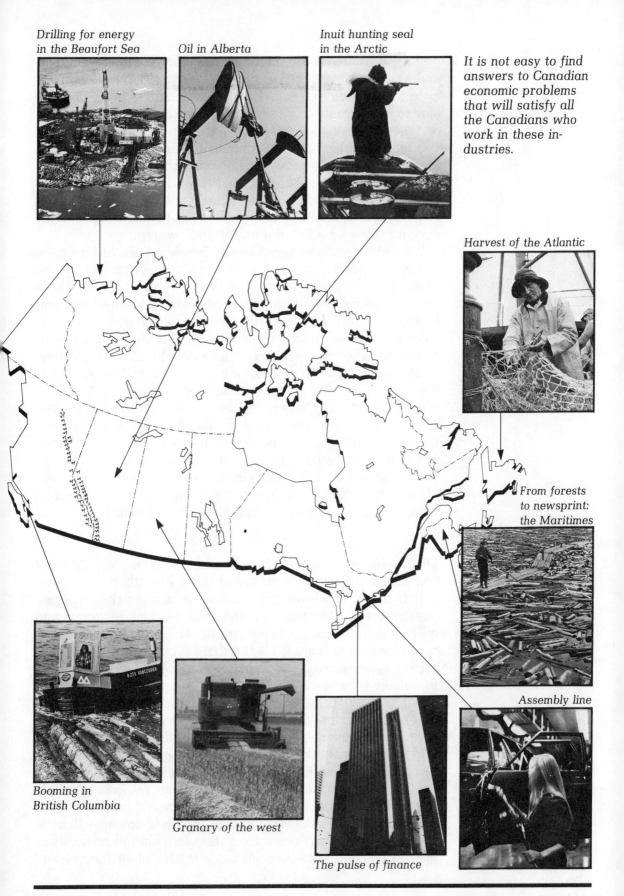

Drilling for energy
in the Beaufort Sea

Oil in Alberta

Inuit hunting seal
in the Arctic

It is not easy to find
answers to Canadian
economic problems
that will satisfy all
the Canadians who
work in these in-
dustries.

Harvest of the Atlantic

From forests
to newsprint:
the Maritimes

Assembly line

Booming in
British Columbia

Granary of the west

The pulse of finance

Other sections of Canada, particularly southern Ontario and Quebec, live mainly by manufacturing. Manufacturers hope to sell their goods largely inside Canada. Many of them look to government to protect their markets by putting tariffs or taxes on foreign goods coming into Canada. These *protective tariffs* enable them to sell their Canadian-made goods for less than imported goods. Whenever economic questions arise, therefore, there are likely to be sharply different views held by the Quebec textile worker, the Ontario automobile worker, the Prairie farmer, the Alberta oil driller, the British Columbia logger and those who fish the icy Atlantic waters.

Many Canadians do not work directly in jobs that produce goods. They work in what are called the service industries. These include shopkeepers, clerks and typists, doctors, lawyers, telephone operators, school teachers and university professors, bankers and insurance salespeople. They provide services rather than goods. Their work, too, is vital to the health of society and the economy. These people, like their fellow Canadians who work in resource industries and manufacturing, also have strong views about the economy. Often their views conflict. Members of the same profession may share the same opinions on matters that directly affect their profession. But often their ideas will be shaped by the region in which they live and by the economic interests of that region. The school teacher in a British Columbia logging camp may agree with the ideas of the workers who are cutting down the trees more than with the views of teachers in Edmonton or Toronto.

Values and Beliefs

Most Canadians believe in, and value, democracy, individual freedom and the rule of law. But there are other values and beliefs about which we differ. Some Canadians are conservative in outlook. They tend to believe that changes in society and government should be made gradually. And they should be made only when there is clear proof that change is really necessary. Other Canadians are more radical in outlook and tend to welcome change. Some Canadians believe that the country's wealth should be shared among its citizens. Others believe that everyone should look after his or her own interests. Some favour religious instruction in schools; others oppose it.

Our values and beliefs are determined in part by our upbringing and the ideas of our parents and relatives. They are shaped as well by our formal education, our religion, our reading, and our observations of the world around us. There is no certain way to predict what values or beliefs anyone will hold. Two Canadians may come from the same kind of home. They may attend the same school, work in the same factory and make the same amount of money. Yet they are almost certain to have different opinions on many questions. When these differences are expressed in words, actions and votes, they have an effect on government in Canada.

"I hope you have the maturity to realize that what we are doing is all for the best."

In every democratic country, governments redistribute the country's wealth. Everyone contributes by paying taxes and everyone receives benefits. Although everyone receives the same benefits, the rich are taxed more heavily to provide them. The extent to which we believe that our wealth should be redistributed is one indication of our political values. What is cartoonist Chambers suggesting?

The basic forces that make up the political environment, then, are geography, history, society, economics, and values and beliefs. The way we think about or react to these forces puts a great deal of energy into that environment. Much of this energy is released in the form of *demands* for some kind of action by government. These may include demands for better roads, new schools, higher old-age pensions, improved medical services, support for troubled industries or professions, lower taxes, greater protection for the rights of individuals and minorities, a stronger stand on a matter of foreign policy. Sometimes demands for action are created by events outside our own political environment. War in the Middle East, or the export to Canada of thousands of foreign cars that seems to threaten our automobile industry are examples. Sometimes political leaders create demands. They make us promises and encourage us to believe that our lives could be much better if we would give them and their parties our support.

Demands for Action

HOW DO OUR DEMANDS REACH GOVERNMENT?

Whatever their origins, demands for government action, or in-action, must be organized if they are to influence the government. One person, no matter how talented or how worthy his or her cause, is not likely to make much of an impact. This is a major problem in a representative, democratic system. How can we make sure that the people we elect to rule on our behalf know what we think about issues? How are they to know what course of action we think they should take? Since one person does not have much power, democratic societies over the years have developed a number of devices or systems of communication. These systems enable groups within a society to gain a collective "clout" that will force governments to listen to them.

Mass Media

The method of communication with which we are likely to be most familiar is the *mass media*. This includes radio, television, newspapers and magazines. Sometimes the mass media is called simply, *the press.* The press not only reveals what people are thinking and what is happening. It also helps to shape public opinion on important issues. As we all know, the press reports the news. But in doing so, it also helps to make it. Continual emphasis on the unemployed does not change the number of people out of work. But it does help to make unemployment an important issue.

In reporting the news and in helping to form public opinion, the press uses many approaches. It sends reporters to interview "people on the street" on important issues or events. It conducts public-opinion polls on questions of interest and concern to Canadians. It repeatedly states that such and such a percentage of the people think that certain actions should or should not be taken. Editorials in newspapers, and on radio and television as well, highlight given issues. They encourage the reader or the listener to come to certain conclusions or to make certain demands on the government. A few politicians claim that they rarely read newspapers or watch television. But most of them and their staffs pay a great deal of attention to the media. Certainly, it is one of the best means by which governments are made aware of the views of the people they represent.

The press also makes sure that information flows in more than one direction. It is through the press that governments let the people know what they are thinking and why they have adopted certain policies.

THIS TIME,
YOU BE A **WON'T SAY** AND
I'LL BE A **DON'T KNOW**.

Public opinion polls are constantly telling us and our governments what we think on every imaginable subject.

Pressure groups are less well known than the mass media. But they are also effective in helping to bridge the gap between the political environment and the people in government who make decisions. As the term suggests, a pressure group is made up of like-minded people who have organized themselves to bring pressure on the government.

There are many kinds of groups. Most have a particular interest to put forward or to protect. They include organizations like the Canadian Medical Association, the Canadian Bankers' Association, the Canadian Manufacturers' Association, trade unions, organizations of small businesses, religious groups, language and cultural groups, and a large number of neighbourhood or community organizations.

Some pressure groups are organized on a permanent basis. They have large staffs that work to make sure that the government is always aware of the wishes and concerns of the group. Other pressure groups are organized for a specific and limited purpose. This might be to prevent the extension of an expressway or the dumping of radioactive waste in their community.

Pressure Groups

Many pressure groups operate quietly and behind closed doors. But often Canadians take to the streets to make their demands known — today and yesterday.

Whatever their goals, all pressure groups use the same sort of tactics to try to get governments to accept their demands. They make their views known in print. They appear on television and radio programs. They hound local politicians and demand interviews with leading cabinet ministers or the prime minister. They plead, they bargain, they threaten. Sometimes they win, sometimes they lose. Seldom is any pressure group ignored by government if it represents a significant bloc of voters or if the group is concerned with an issue that is politically "sensitive," that is, if the issue could lead to a weakening of the party's hold on power.

How lobby groups fared in MacEachen's new budget

● *After the shocks of the November budget, several business groups began an intensive lobbying effort to persuade Ottawa to help them. Although the June 28 budget is still being digested, it's possible to see if the lobbying paid off.*

By Christopher Waddell

FROM THE time the current Liberal government was elected in February, 1980, it has faced an almost constant barrage of criticism of its policies and programs.

First, the introduction of the National Energy Program in October, 1980, produced shockwaves that are still reverberating through the energy industry. Then, just about a year later, the federal budget created an uproar that at times made the attacks on the National Energy Program seem tame by comparison.

Not only its content, but the way the budget was prepared came under assault from the private sector. Suggestions were made, both publicly and privately, on how the budget's detailed provisions and the budgetary process itself should be altered to allow more groups to have a say in its contents.

The first changes came in mid-December, but the pressure on the government continued to the point where Ottawa finally relented in mid-June as Finance Minister Allan MacEachen told the House of Commons he would be introducing a new budget on June 28. That decision came just a month after Energy Minister Marc Lalonde had announced Ottawa's $2-billion assistance package to the financially hard-pressed oil and gas industry.

That NEP Update document was the Energy Department's response to the changed world oil scene, Alberta's industry-assistance program and the petroleum industry's lobbying campaign to soften the tax burden placed on the industry by the NEP. The new federal budget was the Finance Department's reply to the pressure it had faced.

Preparations for the new budget suggested that Finance officials had paid some attention to the criticism that followed last November's effort. The Finance minister noted in his budget speech: "The government has examined very carefully alternative policy options. The actions we have decided to take reflect the broad consensus emerging from the suggestions made by various groups, individuals and Members of Parliament."

But MacEachen also stated that any suggestions made to federal officials had to fall within strict guidelines if there was to be any hope of their being considered by those drafting the budget. The dramatic rise in the deficit left almost no room for new government spending and little opportunity to introduce any new tax concessions that might cut into anticipated federal government revenues.

Within those confines, however, it is possible to look at lobbying efforts made by various industry groups following the last budget, and their success, if any, in getting recognition of their points of view in the new budget.

Canadian Manufacturers' Association

THE CMA is one of the more powerful, consistent and better-known private forces working to mold government policy in Ottawa. Delegations from its varied committees, backed up by staff work from its Toronto headquarters are involved in an all-but-constant round of meetings at the ministerial level, with MPs, with senior civil servants and with opposition party critics.

Even Ottawa, on occasion, comes to it for advice. For instance, CMA President Roy Phillips says his was the first organization chosen by Finance Minister MacEachen when he and cabinet colleagues staged a roadshow to consult with business leaders across the country this past spring.

Prior to the recent budget, the CMA urged Ottawa to continue its fight to beat inflation, while emphasizing that interest rates were devastating to manufacturers. It also called for all governments in Canada to support a restraint program, and pointed out the impact of government-regulated prices in transportation, communication and utilites on the consumer price index.

"I think we've had a telling effect there," Phillips says.

On the other hand, the CMA doesn't appear to have reached federal officials with its concern over investment.

"There seems to be a real blockage in Ottawa on the understanding of the need for investment by industry," Phillips says.

— **Robert English**

Investment Dealers' Association

AFTER MANY — Andrew Kniewasser won't say how many — meetings with senior officials in the Department of Finance and a March 26 meeting with the cabinet, the Investment Dealers' Association claims a number of items in the latest budget as the result of its lobbying.

"We don't use the word lobby. I think lobbyists buy people drinks and take them playing golf, and we don't do that," says IDA President Kniewasser, who was invited to have a drink with Finance Minister MacEachen on budget night.

The IDA asked for measures to stimulate new equity financing in Canada and that business be consulted on any new measures. And it won these points in the latest budget. The association also asked — with some degree of success — for changes in Fira, and that the government stick with its anti-inflation policy. But several other requested measures weren't in the budget.

Now, however, the IDA will be applying new pressure on the government for a quicker reporting date (it is now Sept. 30) for the business committee examining the budget's proposed investment incentives. "We will be pressuring ministers and officials to make it happen sooner," Kniewasser says.

— **Patricia Best**

Small business

WHEN IT comes to influencing federal budget-makers, small-business organizations feel they have been largely shut out by an insular federal bureaucracy.

Pat Johnston, Canadian Federation of Independent Business vice-president, legislative affairs, says the group's immediate post-budget meeting with Finance Minister MacEachen and parliamentary assistant John Evans was "totally fruitless."

"They prepared a press release before the meeting and released it afterward. That set up insularity between us and the government," Johnston explains. "After that, they offered to have us meet with the officials who drafted the original material, but we declined because we knew what reception we would receive."

The CFIB's main post-budget effort was "to rip $250,000 out of our operating budget to generate the information we needed to fight," she adds.

Part of this "fight-back" package was the 113-page *Federal Budget: Report No. 2*, which was distributed across the country and to MPs. Comments on the report were prepared by the Small Business Secretariat, the Department of Finance, and the finance division of Industry, Trade & Commerce, but the CFIB "was never given the courtesy of seeing them, not even if they were only rebuttals."

CFIB lobbyists and members "looked at every conceivable angle and talked to every politician under the sun," Johnston says. Efforts included encouraging questions in the House of Commons, educating journalists about small-business issues, sending *Report No. 2* to accounting firms, and encouraging members to "put the heat on local MPs where they have to get re-elected — and we're going to make sure they don't have a long, lazy summer this year, either."

Johnston says advertising also plays an important role in gaining attention from politicians, since "government can ignore the desires of interest groups, but it can hardly ignore the public impact of interest groups."

Small-business groups feel they have had some influence in encouraging Ottawa to contain public-sector costs. But on the larger, central issues of public confidence and business productivity, there is "total frustration," they say.

Geoffrey Hale, Ontario policy director for the Canadian Organization of Small Business, says the group attempted to meet with both politicians and civil servants developing various pieces of legislation.

Following the November budget, COSB spokesmen met with officials from the Privy Council Office, the departments of Regional Industrial Expansion and Finance, and with Small Business Minister Charles Lapointe. Finance Minister MacEachen "stonewalled" the group's attempts for a meeting, Hale says.

"We spent the months end-running Finance, trying to storm Finance, and talking to anyone and everyone who would listen to us," he says. "We had the distinct impression they were trying to circumvent the business organizations — maybe because small business is thought of as a lost cause as far as political support goes."

Hale says his group was extremely dissatisfied with its attempts to meet Finance officials. As a whole, he says, dealing with bureaucrats is "a waste of time" — yet they are the ones most likely to make technical policy changes. Political lobbying, on the other hand, is a "blunt instrument" to achieve those ends, he says.

"I don't think we've had the impact we've had in Ontario, for instance, in the same circumstances," Hale says. "In Ontario, we've talked to the tax-policy people and the minister both before and after the budget, and it's possible to talk to them without having to break conceptual barriers."

Hale says the COSB now will begin setting up meetings with MacEachen and Finance officials, Small Business Minister Lapointe and members of the consultative committee called for in the budget speech, to register the group's dissatisfaction with the June 28 budget.

— **Marianne Tefft**

Retail Council of Canada

THE COUNCIL has concentrated its efforts since last November on reversing Ottawa's decision to shift the federal sales tax from the manufacturer to the wholesale level. Briefs were submitted to Finance Department officials on this issue with the most recent one going to Allan MacEachen just prior to the latest budget. As well, council representatives have met with opposition critics and Finance Department officials, but not directly with the minister.

Although last month's budget did not mention any possible change to last November's plan to shift the sales tax, the council did achieve a small degree of success when Ottawa decided to make the shift effective Jan. 1, 1983, rather than the originally announced date of July 1, 1982.

— **Frances Phillips**

The Financial Post, *July 17, 1982*

The political party is probably the most important link between the political environment and the government. Within the party are thousands of members from all parts of the country. Many of them are ambitious to win seats and power in provincial or national governments. The party has a staff whose job it is to be aware at all times of public opinion. As a result, the political party is one of the best means by which the people can communicate their views to those who hold public office. Later on, we shall examine more closely the nature and role of political parties in our political system.

Political Parties

Elections

The most dramatic method of communication between the people and the government takes place at elections. In general, elections are held about every four years. Through elections, the voters pass judgement on the political party in power — the government — and compare its performance and promises with those of the other parties who want to replace it in office. Free elections are of central importance in a democracy. They provide the means by which the people can express their discontent and disapproval of government. If they choose, they can vote to change their representatives.

It is worth mentioning again that all of the above methods of communication flow two ways. They enable the people to reach their governments. They also let governments communicate with the people. Through the press, through their responses to pressure groups, through the policies and actions of their political party, and at elections, governments try to explain and to justify their actions.

HOW DO GOVERNMENTS RESPOND?

At the centre of the political system are the people whom we have chosen to represent us. They will make some of the most important decisions affecting our lives. Life is not easy for the *decision-makers*. They must examine major problems facing the country and make plans for their solution on a long-term basis. They must also respond to a multitude of issues and concerns that arise from day to day. Seldom are there simple answers to either long- or short-term problems. A solution to one problem will often create another kind of difficulty. Often the decision-makers do not agree about which problems are most important and which solutions best. This is not surprising in a country like Canada which, as we have seen, is marked by diversity. This diversity makes Canada very hard to govern. Its decision-makers must be always and imaginatively sensitive to the demands that come from all parts of the political environment.

Policies and Regulations

Governments or decision-makers respond in many ways to demands coming from the political environment. Responses may be a statement of policy. Such statements might be that Canada will take a certain stand on a matter of aid to other countries or on the problem of growing tension between the United States and the Soviet Union. Sometimes responses may be no more than changes in some rules and regulations. Examples might include changes to make it easier to pass through customs at border points or airports, or revisions to make income-tax forms simpler to fill out.

"So, what's the good word?"

The decision-makers in the Canadian Cabinet: a much sought-after position in spite of the problems cabinet ministers face

Laws

The most definite and concrete response of decision-makers takes the form of new laws or changes in laws. For example, the government could increase aid to the unemployed, raise or lower taxes, limit foreign investment, fix prices and wages, give aid to home owners, or provide increased support for farmers.

Each response by the government changes the political environment. If we are satisfied, we forget about that demand. We shift our attention to other matters and develop new demands. If we are displeased, we may try to increase the pressure on government in support of our demand. Or we may change the nature of our protest. Changes in the political environment caused by various kinds of government responses show the living nature of our political system. Each response marks an end and a beginning in the continuous life cycle that marks the political environment. Thus the process of change and development continues without interruption. The political system, with government at its centre, is very much alive.

Getting the Facts

1. Define the following: politics, political system, geography, history, economy, value, conservative, liberal, radical, diverse, region, political environment, political party, pressure group, mass media, natural resource, foreign policy, foreign investment, tariff, policy.

2. In what ways do the following affect Canada's political system: geography, history, society, the economy, values and beliefs?

3. How do the Canadian people communicate with their governments and vice versa?

Using the Facts

1. From your own experience if possible, give examples to show both the good and the bad effects of such forces as geography, history, society, the economy, values and beliefs on our political system.

2. Which of the forces named in Question 1 do you think has had the strongest effect on Canada in the past? Today? Explain your answer.

3. It has been said that in order to understand Canada, it is necessary to understand its regions. What does this statement mean? Do you agree with it?

4. Which of the methods of communication between the people and the government do you think is most effective? Why?

5. Are pressure groups common? List as many pressure groups as you can that are not mentioned in the text. How do they apply pressure? Do you think their activities are good or bad? Do you have any pressure groups at school?

6. In a later chapter, we will examine the role of the press in detail. At this stage, can you suggest some problems related to the press that may arise in a democratic society?

7. We shall also look more closely at political parties later in the book. Can you suggest now some of the problems political parties are likely to face as they try to win and keep power?

8. There is some criticism of the extensive use of public opinion polls before elections. The argument runs that the results of these polls, indicating that one party has a large lead over the others, influence how we decide to vote. Do you agree? Should polls be stopped two weeks before an election?

1. (a) Research the events illustrated on the map on pages 24-5. **Research Projects**
   (b) How have these events influenced our views of Canadian history and helped to shape the political environment today?
   (c) How have events in your locality influenced your view of Canadian history?
2. Attempt to determine how Canadians engaged in the activities in the photographs on page 27 would feel about the following economic policies: tariff protection against manufactured goods from other countries; higher taxes on wages; higher taxes on company profits; a reduction in financial support given to farmers. Can you think of one policy on which all might agree? Or disagree?
3. Do governments respond to pressure? During the next month, record as many examples as you can find of governments responding to some kind of pressure. Indicate the source of the pressure, the nature of the government response, and the way in which you learned of the situation. What are your thoughts or conclusions about pressure groups at the end of the month?
4. (a) What economic policies would the people illustrated on the map on page 27 demand that the government follow?
   (b) Identify different economic groups in your community. Suggest five pictures illustrating the most important economic activities.
   (c) What economic policies would each of the five demand that the government follow?

Chapter 3
HOW DOES DEMOCRACY WORK?

Who Can Vote?
Votes for Women
Universal Suffrage

Are All Votes Equal?
Distribution
Equal Representation?

Does the Majority Rule?
Our Multi-party System

How Are Elections Held?
The Secret Ballot
An Election

Who Can Run? Who Does Run?
Women in Politics

The leaders of Ontario's political parties and the King for a Day, 1972

About five hundred years before the birth of Christ, the little Greek city-state of Athens became the world's first democracy. To modern Canadians, this early Greek form of democratic government would seem strange. For in Athens the people actually did rule — at least the 40 000 males who were citizens ruled. To an Athenian citizen it was unthinkable that someone else should govern for him. Democracy in Athens meant that all of the citizens could make their own laws directly.

As we have seen, democratic government in Canada is not *direct* democracy of the Greek sort. It is clearly not possible for all the citizens in any modern state to govern themselves directly. In a modern democracy like Canada, the people "rule" by choosing others to act for, or represent, them in government. Thus Canada has a *representative* as opposed to a direct form of democracy.

There must be an election every five years. Usually, however, a government in power "goes to the people" before the end of the five-year term. When a government waits the full five years, it is a sign that the government does not think its chances of re-election are very good. When this cartoon was published in August 1972, Prime Minister Trudeau had been in office for more than four years. He faced the people two months later and narrowly escaped defeat. In 1979, Trudeau did go "to the end of his rope" and lost the election.

As Confucius might have said "Man who keeps going to end of his rope succeeds only in tightening noose."

In Canada, the voters elect representatives to the House of Commons. To arrange for the election of such members to the Commons, the country is organized into 282 geographical areas known as *constituencies*. The more common name for constituency is a riding or a seat. In each riding, the different political parties choose candidates to run for election. On election day, the candidate who receives the largest number of votes is elected. The candidate takes a seat in the House of Commons to represent the people of that riding. Under normal circumstances, the party that wins the most ridings will form the government. The leader of the winning party will become the prime minister. Therefore, we vote not only for a candidate, but also for a political party and for a prime minister.

In ancient Athens, each of the 40 000 citizens participated directly in government. In 1981, our 11 000 000 Canadian voters elected 282 citizens to represent them — exactly one representative for every 40 000 voters — and one prime minister to speak for eleven million!

WHO CAN VOTE?

Today in national elections every man and woman who is eighteen or over and is a Canadian citizen has the *franchise*, or the right to vote. Members of the armed forces may vote regardless of age. Denied the right to vote are judges, the civil servants who supervise the elections, criminals, lunatics, and people found guilty of dishonest practices in previous elections.

Until the twentieth century, it seemed to be assumed, at least by men, that only men should have the right to vote. In their struggle for the right to vote, women in Canada did not interrupt debates in Parliament. Nor did they chain themselves to lampposts, put acid in mailboxes, or throw themselves under racehorses, as was the case in England. But if their methods were less dramatic, Canadian women were no less determined. One of the most effective was Nellie McClung, one of the leaders of the Votes for Women Movement in Manitoba. In 1914, twenty years after women first asked for the vote, she urged Premier Roblin to give women the vote. Roblin gently refused and would not let her speak to his Cabinet:

Votes for Women

Even if they listened to you, which I doubt, you would upset them and I don't want that to happen. They are good fellows: they do what they are told. Every government has to have a head and I am the head of this one and I don't want any dissensions and arguments. You can't come here and make trouble for my boys just when I have them trotting easy and eating out of my hand. Now you forget all this nonsense about women voting. You're a fine, smart young woman, I can see that. And take it from me, nice women don't want to vote.

Roblin continued to attack the Votes for Women movement as one backed only "by men who wear long hair and women who wear short hair." But the movement led by Nellie McClung was successful. Women in Manitoba got the vote in 1916. By 1922, all other provinces, except Quebec, had fol-

THE UPHILL BATTLE FOR THE RIGHT TO VOTE

Nellie McClung was one of a group of determined women in western Canada who fought for the vote — and for such other causes as an end to the sale of liquor. Born in Ontario, she moved to Manitoba where she became a teacher. Nellie McClung was perhaps the most popular "suffragette" and filled Massey Hall when she spoke in Toronto. In 1921 she was elected to the Alberta legislature. Just a few months earlier Mary Ellen Smith had become the first woman cabinet minister when she was appointed to the British Columbia Cabinet.

(Left) Many male politicians not only opposed women's suffrage, but argued that most women did not want the vote. The cartoon shows Premier Walter Scott of Saskatchewan asking women to speak up if they really want the vote.

(Right) The first woman to be elected to the House of Commons was Agnes Macphail. An Ontario school teacher, Macphail was elected first as a member of the United Farmers of Ontario.

DO NOT FAIL TO HEAR
Mrs. Nellie L. McClung
LECTURE
On Woman Suffrage, Temperance Issues and Things Political.

AN OPEN DISCUSSION IS DESIRED

Mrs. McClung is acknowledged to be one of the foremost platform speakers in the west to-day.

THE TOWN HALL, KILLARNEY
THURSDAY, JUNE THE 18TH
AT EIGHT O'CLOCK SHARP

Reserved Seats 35c.   General Admission 25c.
Plan of Hall at Evans' Drug Store.

SPEAK!

VOTES FOR WOMEN

At the last session of the Saskatchewan Legislature Premier Scott expressed himself as in favor of extending the franchise to women, but did not care to enact the necessary legislation until the women of Saskatchewan asked for it. It is now up to the women to "SPEAK" in clear and unmistakable terms.

From Grain Growers' Guide, February 26, 1913

lowed Manitoba's example. In 1918, the federal government gave women the right to vote. Not until 1940, however, were women allowed to vote in Quebec provincial elections.

Women were not the only Canadians who did not have the right to vote. Until late in the nineteenth century, men could not vote unless they owned property or paid rent. It was not until 1948 that all Canadians of Asian parentage had the right to vote. The Inuit received the vote only in 1950. And it was as late as 1960 that all Canadian Indians on reservations were allowed to vote.

Universal Suffrage

In many countries in the modern world, men and women have died in their attempt to gain a democratic system where they may vote freely. In Canada today, one third of those who have the right to vote in national and provincial elections fail to do so. In municipal elections, the figure is sometimes as high as two thirds. Some countries have made voting compulsory. Should we?

ARE ALL VOTES EQUAL?

Very few of us would question the basic democratic principle that the vote of every person should count for the same. One voter should equal one vote. Here we have a major difficulty. In Canada, the simple truth is that every vote does not have equal weight. There is a gap between the democratic ideal of equality and actual political practice.

Distribution

The 282 federal constituencies in Canada are distributed according to population. The number of people in the country are counted every ten years in a census. Each province is then given the number of seats that roughly corresponds to the share of the total population of Canada. Thus each province is represented fairly. The same cannot be said about the constituencies.

One would expect that each riding would have roughly the same number of voters. Only then would every vote have equal weight. But such is not the case. Before the federal ridings were reformed in 1966, three had fewer than 12 000 people and several had more than 200 000. This same imbalance could be found in the distribution of seats for the provincial legislatures. In general, the less settled rural areas were over-represented when compared to the rapidly growing cities.

In recent years, however, there has been great progress in improving the representative system. In 1963, for the first

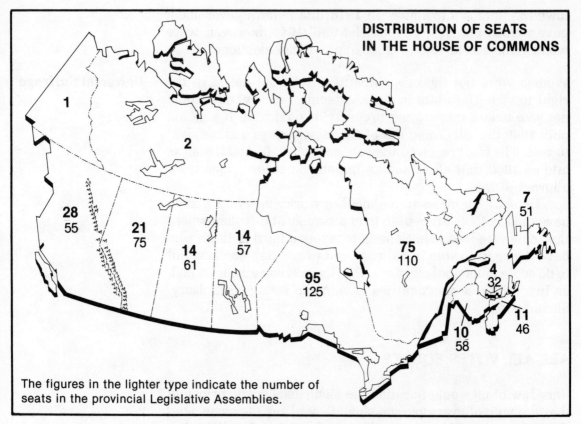

DISTRIBUTION OF SEATS IN THE HOUSE OF COMMONS

1

2

28
55

21
75

14
61

14
57

95
125

75
110

7
51

4
32

10
58

11
46

The figures in the lighter type indicate the number of seats in the provincial Legislative Assemblies.

time in Canadian history, the government in Ottawa appointed an independent commission to carry out a thorough redistribution of seats. (Before, governments had rearranged the constituencies themselves. Usually, they had been justly accused of arranging the boundaries so as to improve their own prospects and to hurt those of their opponents.) In 1963, the members of the commission were told that they were not to let the size of ridings vary more than twenty-five per cent. When the commission reported in 1965, few ridings in Canada remained the same.

Although the 1966 redistribution improved matters, it still did not create ridings of equal population. The cities, on the whole, remained under-represented. Montreal, Toronto, Vancouver, and Winnipeg still sent fewer members to Ottawa than their populations warranted. In the federal election of 1979, for example, 81 000 people voted in York-Scarborough. Forty-five thousand voted in Vancouver Centre. Only 28 000 went to the polls in Gaspé, Quebec.

Equal Representation?

Why not make all ridings exactly the same? The opponents of equal representation raise two main objections. They argue that rural citizens are likely to be property owners. Their personal roots, like those of their crops, lie deep in the soil of the country. As a result, the argument runs, they have a greater stake in their community. They will take their political duties more seriously than the rootless wage earners of the city. Decades ago, before Canada was industrialized and most Canadians lived in cities, this argument may have carried some weight. It does not today.

The second argument against equal representation is stronger. If all ridings were equal in population, some rural and northern ridings would be huge. It would be difficult, if not impossible, for their representatives to travel through the ridings, meet the people they represent, and get to know their problems. As a result, many Canadians would feel they were cut off from their government.

DOES THE MAJORITY RULE?

Most Canadians accept the principle that in a democracy the government should represent a majority of citizens. In other words, the majority should rule. Once again, a glance beneath the surface shows a gap between principle and practice. It has often happened in Canada and elsewhere that the government represents the choice of fewer than half the voters who went to the polls. Moreover, the number of seats a political party holds in the House of Commons often does not reflect the number of votes the party received. How does this happen?

Imagine for a moment that in each riding only two candidates, a Liberal and a Conservative, are running. Imagine, too, that in every riding the Liberal candidate received only one vote less than the Conservative. The Liberals would win no seats. The Conservatives, with a total of only 282 votes more than the Liberals, would hold every seat in the House of Commons. The example, of course, is absurd. But seats have been won by one vote. A margin of one vote is as good as one of ten thousand in winning an election.

The fact that three, four, or even five parties may run candidates in an election also makes it difficult for the principle of majority rule to work. With the vote split many ways, the winner often gets fewer than half the votes. (In the federal election of 1980, for example, almost half of those elected in Ontario and all of those elected in Saskatchewan were supported by less than 50% of the voters.) Visitors from non-democratic states might question some of our democratic principles when they see cases in which 65% of the voters in a riding

Our Multi-party System

In some elections, the percentage of votes received and the percentage of seats won is fairly close. In many cases, no party wins a majority of seats. In such circumstances, the prime minister or premier leads what is called "a minority government." When did we have minority governments in Ottawa? In Ontario? In British Columbia?

Our system also results in changes in the number of seats won in the House of Commons or the provincial assemblies that are much greater than the change in public opinion would indicate. For example, in the federal election of 1980 the Liberals gained only 3% more of the popular vote than they won in 1979. Yet they gained 12% more of the seats and easily won a majority. In Ontario in 1981, the Conservatives gained only 4% more of the popular vote than in 1977. But they won an astonishing number of additional seats. Looking only at the figures, what might explain the results in British Columbia since 1969?

PERCENTAGE OF TOTAL VOTES RECEIVED COMPARED WITH PERCENTAGE OF NUMBER OF SEATS WON

FEDERAL ELECTIONS, 1958-1980

	Liberals		Conservatives		C.C.F. & NDP		Social Credit	
Year	% Votes	% Seats	% Votes	% Seats	% Votes	% Seats	% Votes	% Seats
1958	33	18	54	79	10	3	2	0
1962	37	38	37	44	13	7	12	11
1963	41	49	33	36	14	6	12	9
1965	40	49	32	37	18	8	9	5
1968	45	59	31	27	17	8	6	6
1972	39	41	35	41	18	12	8	6
1974	42	53	35	36	15	6	5	4
1979	40	40	36	48	18	9	5	2
1980	43	52	33	36	20	11	2	0

ONTARIO, 1971-1981

	Liberals		Conservatives		NDP	
Year	% Votes	% Seats	% Votes	% Seats	% Votes	% Seats
1971	28	17	45	67	27	16
1975	34	29	36	41	29	30
1977	31	27	40	46	28	26
1981	34	34	44	70	21	21

BRITISH COLUMBIA, 1969-1979

	Social Credit		NDP		Liberals		Conservatives	
Year	% Votes	% Seats	% Votes	% Seats	% Votes	% Seats	% Votes	% Seats
1969	69	47	22	34	9	19	0	0
1972	18	32	69	39	10	16	4	13
1975	64	49	33	39	2	7	2	4
1979	54	48	47	46	0	4	0	5

have voted against the person who won the seat and who will represent the riding in Parliament!

In short, as a result of the way in which our democratic system actually works, it is possible that the number of seats held by a party in the House of Commons or the provincial Legislative Assembly may not fairly reflect the party's strength among the people. The tables opposite show the percentage of the total votes received compared with the percentage of the number of seats won in some recent elections. They show clearly the gap between the principle of majority rule and what has happened in practice. How many governments have received the support of a majority of the voters?

The election of 1980 raises another serious question. Five hundred and fifty-five thousand out of a total of about 2 500 000 voters in the provinces of British Columbia, Alberta and Saskatchewan voted for Liberal candidates. Yet not one Liberal in these provinces received enough votes to win a seat. Similarly, 373 300 out of 2 994 000 voters in Quebec cast votes for the Conservative Party. Just one Conservative was elected. In other words, Liberal voters in the three western provinces and Conservative voters in Quebec were almost totally unrepresented in the House of Commons. Such a situation does not help national unity.

There are many ways to ensure a closer fit between the votes received and the seats won. While some of them are very complicated, it is interesting that fifteen of the nineteen Western democratic countries have adopted some other system that they believe is more democratic than the system we use. Only Great Britain, the United States and New Zealand have the same system as we do. Many believe it is time we joined the majority. Do you?

HOW ARE ELECTIONS HELD?

Holding an election is a complicated matter. It involves the efforts of a great many citizens. From the time an election is announced until the votes are counted and the victors named, an elaborate process is in operation. Every step in this process (see pages 48-9) is designed to ensure a fair, honest and efficient election.

The secret ballot is essential in a democracy. In 1867, when Canada was formed, voting was carried on by word of mouth or by a show of hands. The system was open to many abuses. Some employers, for example, threatened employees who did

The Secret Ballot

Toronto Star front page, Friday December 14, 1979 — "HERE WE GO AGAIN / Election Feb. 18 as PCs fall"

PRELIMINARY LIST OF ELECTORS — LISTE PRÉLIMINAIRE DES ÉLECTEURS — ELECTIONS CANADA

1. Amon, Gary (m) RRA Barrie LAM 456
2. Amon, Eleanor (f) RRA Barrie LAM 456
3. Amon, Kimberley (f) RRA Barrie LAM 456
4. Amon, Dorothy (f) RRA Barrie LAM 456
5. Annett, Grace F. (f) RR1 Stroud LOL 2M0
6. Arnett, Grace S. (f) RR1 Stroud LOL 2M0
7. Ashton, Barry (m) RRA Barrie LAM 456
8. Ashton, Melanie (f) RRA Barrie LAM 456
9. Apea, Peter (m) RRA Barrie LAM 456
10. Apea, Valda (f) RRA Barrie LAM 456
11. Bowman, John (m) RR1 Stroud LOL 2M0
12. Bowman, Helen (f) RR1 Stroud LOL 2M0
13. Brice, Richard (m) RR1 Stroud LOL 2M0
14. Brice, Linda (f) RR1 Stroud LOL 2M0
15. Black, Alex (m) RRA Barrie LAM 456
16. Blaney Gerald (m) RRA Barrie LA6 46
17. Blaney, Linda (f) RRA Barrie LAM 456
18. Blight, Raymond (m) RR1 Stroud LOL 2M0
19. Blight, Vera (f) RR1 Stroud LOL 2M0
20. Beach, Dalton (m) RR1 Stroud LOL 2M0
21. Beach, Rosemarie (f) RR1 Stroud LOL 2M0
22. Basta, David (m) RR1 Stroud LOL 2M0
23. Basta, Stan. (m) RR1 Stroud LOL 2M0
24. Birch, Gunnar (m) RRA Barrie LAM 456
25. Birch, Allan (m) RRA Barrie LAM 456
26. Birch, Patricia (f) RRA Barrie LAM 456
27. Bebbington, Walter (m) RRA Barrie LAM 456
28. Bebbington, Ada (f) RR1 Stroud LAM 456
29. Brocklebank, Glover (m) RRA Barrie LAM 456
30. Brocklebank, Violet (f) RRA Barrie LAM 456
31. Brocklebank, Anre (f) RRA Barrie LAM 456
32. Ball, Eric (m) RRA Barrie LAM 456
33. Catling, Douglas (m) RR1 Stroud LOL 2M0
34. Catling, Mary (f) RR1 Stroud LOL 2M0
35. Catling, John F. (m) RR1 Stroud LOL 2M0
36. Catling, Timothy (m) RR1 Stroud LOL 2M0
37. Crawford, Wm. (m) 254 Yonge St. RR1 Stroud LOL 2M0
38. Crawford, Chirriu (f) 254 Yonge St. RR1 Stroud LOL 2M0
39. Carducci, Robert (M) Box 51 Stroud, RRA Barrie LAM 456
40. Carducci, Victoria (f) Box 51 Stroud RRA Barrie LAM 456
41. Diceman, Arthur (m) RR1 Stroud LOL 2M0
42. Diceman, Grace (f) RR1 Stroud LOL 2M0
43. Diceman, Garry (m) RR1 Stroud LOL 2M0
44. Durkee, George (m) RR1 Stroud LOL 2M0
45. Durkee, Shirley (f) RR1 Stroud LOL 2M0
46. Darkee, Donna (f) RR1 Stroud LOL 2M0
47. Durkee, Wm. (m) RR1 Stroud LOL 2M0
48. Durkee, Barbara (f) RR1 Stroud LOL 2M0
49. Davies, Wm. (m) 240 Yonge St. RR1 Stroud LOL 2M0
50. Davies, Madeline (f) 240 Yonge St. RR1 Stroud LOL 2M0
51. Dodge, Barbara (f) RRA Barrie LAM 456
52. Diano, Joyce (f) RRA Barrie LAM 456
53. Diano, Salvator (m) RRA Barrie LAM 456
54. Enns, Dorsey (m) RR1 Stroud LOL 2M0
55. Enns, Ina (f) RR1 Stroud LOL 2M0
56. Enns, Jenifer (f) RR1 Stroud LOL 2M0
57. Easby, Muriel (f) RR1 Stroud LOL 2M0
58. Easby, Harold (m) RR1 Stroud LOL 2M0
59. Easby, George (m) RR1 Stroud LOL 2M0
60. Eydt, Eileen (f) RRA Barrie LAM 456
61. Eydt, Samuel (m) RRA Barrie LAM 456
62. Eydt, George (m) RRA Barrie LAM 456
63. Elliott, Robert (m) RRA Barrie LAM 456
64. Fellows, Kenneth (m) RR1 Stroud LOL 2M0
65. Fellows, Norah (f) RR1 Stroud LOL 2M0
66. Fellows, Wesley (m) RR1 Stroud LOL 2M0
67. Fralick, Douglas Sr. (m) 197 Mapleview Dr. RR1 Stroud LOL 2M0
68. Fralick, Joan (f) 197 Mapleview Dr. RR1 Stroud LOL 2M0
69. Freethy, Gordon (m) RRA Barrie LAM 456
70. Freethy, Lisell (f) RRA Barrie LAM 456
71. Freethy, Faye (f) RRA Barrie LAM 456
72. Furaman, Harold (m) RRA Barrie LAM 456
73. Furaman, Marie (f) RRA Barrie LAM 456
74. Farquhar, John (m) RRA Barrie LAM 456
75. Farquhar, Phyllis (f) RRA Barrie LAM 456
76. Graham, Bruce (m) RRA Barrie LAM 456
77. Graham, Brenda (f) RRA Barrie LAM 456
78. Graham, Forbes. (m) RRA Barrie LAM 456
79. Graham, Belle (f) RRA Barrie LAM 456
80. Guest, Myrna (f) 248 Yonge St. RR1 Stroud LOL 2M0
81. Gilroy, Robert (m) RRA Barrie LAM 456
82. Gilroy, Joan. (f) RRA Barrie LAM 456
83. Gallagher, Gerry (m) RRA Barrie LAM 456
84. Ghosh, Sam (m) RRA Barrie LAM 456
85. Ghosh, Trudy (f) RRA Barrie LAM 456
86. Hebert, Murray (m) RR1 Stroud LOL 2M0
87. Hebert, Peggy (f) RR1 Stroud LOL 2M0
88. Hazelden, Robert (m) RR1 Stroud LOL 2M0
89. Hazelden, Valerie (f) RR1 Stroud LOL 2M0
90. Hazelden, Rosalin (f) RR1 Stroud LOL 2M0
91. Hardison, Edward (m) RRA Barrie LAM 456
92. Hardison, Anita (f) RRA Barrie LAM 456
93. Halkes, Wm. (m) RRA Barrie LAM 456
94. Halkes, Lorraine (f) RRA Barrie LAM 456
95. Halkes, Linda (f) RRA Barrie LAM 456
96. Hutchinson, John (m) RRA Barrie LAM 456
97. Hutchinson, Eleanor (f) RRA Barrie LAM 456
98. Harrison, Fred (m) Box 58 Stroud LOL 2M0
99. Hayes, John W. (m) RRA Barrie LAM 456
100. Hayes, Anne O. (f) RRA Barrie LAM 456
101. Hopkins, Harold (m) RRA Barrie LAM 456
102. Hopkins, Heather (f) RRA Barrie LAM 456
103. Jennett, Heart (m) RRA Barrie LAM 456
104. Jennett, Luella (f) RRA Barrie LAM 456
105. Jensen, James (m) RRA Barrie LAM 456
106. Jensen, JoAnne (f) RRA Barrie LAM 456
107. Julian, George (m) RRA Barrie LAM 456
108. Jennings, Maureen (f) RRA Barrie LAM 456
109. Jennings, Thomas (m) RRA Barrie LAM 456
110. Jennings, Lauren (f) RRA Barrie LAM 456
111. Juffermans, Nic (m) RRA Barrie LAM 456

1. A defeat in the House of Commons on December 13, 1979, forced Prime Minister Clark to call an election. Usually, however, the prime minister decides when an election is best for the party. The prime minister advises the Governor General to dissolve Parliament and have an election. Then, an order goes to the chief electoral officer (the civil servant in charge of the election machinery) to put the election machinery in motion.

2. The chief electoral officer sends out to the returning officers (the officials responsible for the election in each constituency) instructions to publish the dates for nomination of candidates and voting. The returning officer divides the constituency into polling stations, or voting locations, one for every 250 voters. The returning officer has a list made up and published of all people entitled to vote.

3. Anyone who can vote and who deposits $200 to show serious intent can be a candidate. The deposit is returned if the candidate receives half as many votes as the winner. Nomination meetings may be hard-fought battles between a number of candidates. Sometimes the party leaders use their influence to have a certain person nominated. Here, two senators and a cabinet minister congratulate Jim Coutts after he won the Liberal nomination in Toronto's Spadina riding in a 1981 by-election.

Polling station

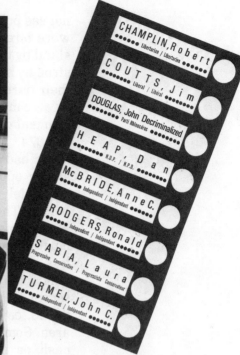

The ballot for the by-election in Spadina riding in Toronto, August 22, 1981.

4. On election day each poll is supervised by a deputy returning officer. The voters enter the polling station, give their names and receive a ballot. They mark the ballot secretly and hand it to the deputy returning officer who places it in a box. When the polls close, the boxes are opened and the ballots counted.

5. By midnight the results are usually fairly well decided in favour of one candidate.

not see politics "in the right light." Sometimes gangs of toughs were hired to make life unpleasant for men brave enough to stand by their opinions. Priests and ministers sometimes felt so strongly about an election that they used threats to persuade their parishioners to vote as they wanted.

To increase the voter's freedom of choice, the Liberal government of Alexander Mackenzie introduced the secret ballot in 1874. This was just two years after Prime Minister Gladstone had done so in England. In both countries there was strong opposition to the change from open to secret voting. Many felt that no man should be ashamed of his political beliefs. They agreed with Sir John A. Macdonald that voting in secret was "un-British." But shame and fear, as Macdonald must have known, are very different things. More honest, if less common, was the frank admission that the secret ballot would cut at the root of political corruption — the open or secret bribing of voters. Before the secret ballot was introduced, candidates knew what a vote was worth in any given area. Some voters held out for a high price, whether it was in cash or merchandise. But with a secret ballot, how was anyone to know for certain if the bribed man had voted as he had promised?

Bribery of the individual voter seldom happens now. But critics of our political system ask whether there is much difference between a cash payment to a voter and the promise of a new post office, a better pension, or lower taxes.

WHO CAN RUN? WHO DOES RUN?

As a general rule, anyone who can vote can also run for election to the House of Commons or the provincial legislatures. We might expect, as a result, that membership in the Commons and the provincial legislatures would reflect the make-up of the population. This is not the case. All studies of those who run for office in Canada or who are elected indicate that people with university educations account for well over half. Yet people with university educations number about ten per cent of the population. Between 1940 and 1960, lawyers accounted for about one third of all members of the House of Commons. Many other members were in the other professions. Yet lawyers and other professionals made up only a small fraction of the population. People who come from non-British or non-French backgrounds also seem not to be represented in proportion to their numbers.

Flora MacDonald, Secretary of State for External Affairs, en route to the Commonwealth Conference in Lusaka, August 1979.

Women in Politics

The next most striking imbalance exists with regard to women. Women have had the right to run for office since they received the vote over sixty years ago. Yet as the report of the *Royal Commission on the Status of Women* observed in 1970, of the 6845 people elected in federal and provincial elections between 1917 and 1970, only 67 were women.

The situation is improving gradually in politics, as in other areas. Between the years 1920 and 1970, for example, there were only 18 women elected in total to the House of Commons. Forty-nine were elected to the provincial legislatures. In the summer of 1982, there were 15 women in the Commons and 49 among the 670 members of the provincial legislatures. But 7% of the total is still far from a reasonable representation of half the Canadian population.

Largely as a result of pressure from women, it is now assumed that there will be women in every federal and provincial Cabinet. The first woman, Ellen Fairclough, was appointed to the federal Cabinet by Prime Minister John Diefenbaker in 1957. With the exception of the years from 1968 to 1972, there have been women in the federal Cabinet ever since. In 1982 there were two, and the Honourable Jeanne Sauvé, who was in the Cabinet from 1972 to 1979, was then

MODERN POLITICAL PIONEERS

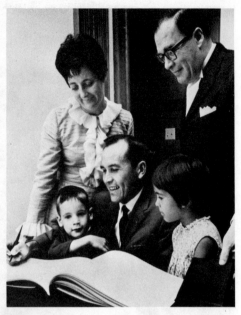

(Above) Jeanne Sauvé, MP, the first woman Speaker in the House of Commons

(Right) Leonard Marchand, the first Canadian Indian to be elected to the House of Commons, signs the oath of allegiance in 1968.

(Left) Leadership candidate Rosemary Brown and her rival for the NDP leadership listen to a third candidate at the leadership convention in 1975.

(Above) The first Inuit to be elected to the House of Commons was Peter Ittinuar, who won in Nunatsiaq in 1979.

(Left) Bertha Wilson sworn in as the first woman member of the Supreme Court of Canada, 1982.

the first woman Speaker of the House of Commons. Women have also been Speakers in the provincial assemblies. Nancy Hodges was appointed Speaker in British Columbia in 1949, the first woman in the Commonwealth to hold the position. In 1982 there were also women cabinet ministers in every province but Nova Scotia and Prince Edward Island.

There may be many reasons why fewer women run for office than do men. Yet even in the appointed Senate they are under-represented. The British North America Act stated that any qualified "person" could be a member of the Senate. Until 1929, the word "person" apparently did not include women. Only then did the highest court in the British Commonwealth decide that a person could be a woman when it came to membership in the Canadian Senate! The first woman was appointed to the Senate in 1930. But in the early 1980s, there were still only 9 women among the 104 members of the Senate.

We have not yet had a woman as prime minister or premier. The first step, of course, is to be elected as leader of a political party. Several women have come close. In 1975, Rosemary Brown, a member of the British Columbia Legislative Assembly, was narrowly defeated for the federal New Democratic Party leadership by Edward Broadbent. A year later, Flora MacDonald unsuccessfully ran for the leadership of the federal Conservatives. She later became Secretary of State for External Affairs in the Clark government, the highest Cabinet position yet to be held by a woman in federal politics. One woman has won the party leadership; today the lone woman in the Nova Scotia legislature, Alexa McDonough, is the leader of the provincial New Democratic Party. In all probability, it will only be a matter of time before Canada joins Great Britain in having a woman as prime minister or provincial premier.

STUDY GUIDE

Getting the Facts

1. Define the following: representative government, constituency, riding, party, franchise, prime minister, majority, redistribution, bribery, suffragette, conscription, urban, secret ballot, candidate, nomination.
2. Who may vote in a federal election?
3. Why are judges not allowed to vote?
4. Why do the votes of all Canadians not have equal weight? How successful have Canadian goverments been in correcting the problem? Explain the advantages and disadvantages of equal representation. Where do you stand?
5. Canadians describe democracy as a system of government in which the majority rules. Why have the governments of Canada so seldom represented a majority of voters?
6. On a simple chart, outline the steps followed from the selection of a candidate to his/her election.
7. How is the secret ballot supposed to prevent corruption?

Using the Facts

1. Should citizens be forced to vote whether they want to or not?
2. Would you be in favour of making citizens pass a test on Canadian government and public affairs before they are allowed to vote? Why?
3. What is the difference between a majority government and a minority government? Which do you think provides the best government? Why?
4. Explain the importance of Nellie McClung in Canadian history. Prepare short reports on other Canadian women who have played important roles in Canada.
5. Using the statistical data in the tables on page 46 which results do you think were the fairest? What is fair?

Research Projects

1. Canadians did not all gain the right to vote at the same time. Trace the stages in the achievement of "universal suffrage" in Canada by finding out when the right to vote was given to different groups in the population. Chart your results on a timeline. In each case, explain why the vote was given at that time.
2. In 1928 the Supreme Court of Canada ruled that women could not be members of the Senate. A year later the Judicial Committee of the Privy Council overturned this decision. Why did this case go to the Supreme Court? Clue: Nellie McClung and Emily Murphy were involved.

3. Why do the opposition parties have more power when the government is in a minority? What demands did each of the opposition party leaders make of the minority Trudeau government between 1972 and 1974? From research, discover whether the opposition parties succeeded in changing the minority Liberal government's actions or policies in these years. Why did Mr. Trudeau finally call an election in 1974? As the headlines on page 48 reveal, the Clark government was defeated in 1979 when one of the smaller parties refused to support it. What was the issue? The result?
4. Many Canadians believe that our system of representative government needs to be changed so that the members we elect will represent a majority of voters. Find out what suggestions have been made for changing the system. How would you suggest we improve the system? Or would you leave it as it is?

Chapter 4
WHY POLITICAL PARTIES?

What Does a Political Party Stand For?
Power
Issues
Middle of the Road

How Are Political Parties Organized?
Organization
Finances
Financial Reform

How Important Is the Party Leader?
Leadership Qualities
Modern Leaders

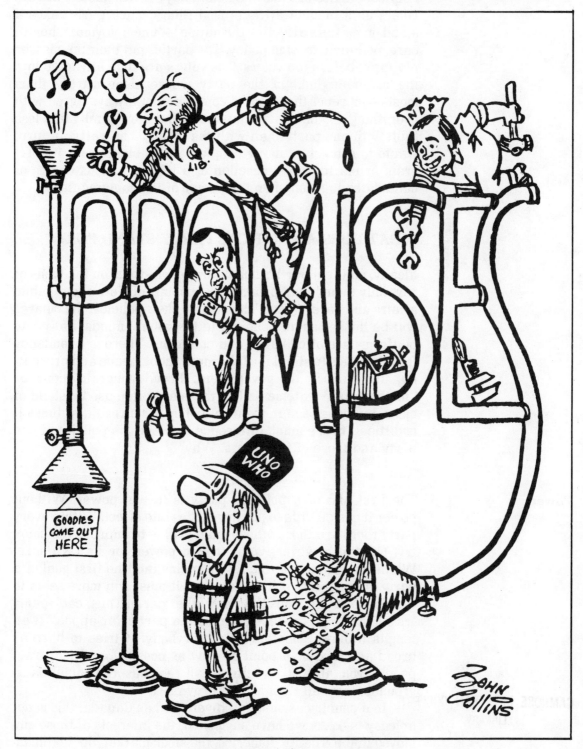

THE ELECTION MACHINE

Political parties are like magnets. They are designed to attract voters as a magnet attracts iron filings. Each party takes a stand on matters affecting the nation — unemployment, health care, pollution, foreign policy. The parties put their policies, or *platform*, before the voters. The voters are then attracted into the magnetic field of the party whose ideas attract them most — or repel them least. Voters do not always agree with everything any one party stands for. But they usually find less fault with one party than with the others. The party, in turn, wants to attract as many people as possible. It uses its program or platform, its selection of a leader, and its choice of candidates to strengthen the power of its magnetic field.

WHAT DOES A POLITICAL PARTY STAND FOR?

Ideally, political parties should try to win votes on the basis of carefully thought-out principles, or points of view about public affairs and government. The clearer their policies, the clearer will be the issues and choices in the voters' minds. But party platforms are often vague and confusing. There is a tendency for all parties to stand for full employment, peace and prosperity, and honesty in government. Broad generalizations or "motherhood" statements like these are often used instead of clear and concise statements of policy. As a result, at times it is difficult to see much difference between the policies of one party and those of the others. Why?

Power

The first aim of a political party is to win power. Without power it can do little to put its policies into effect. Within every party there are those whose main goal is to improve the country. Others, however, want to win power for its own sake. Whatever the motive, the fact remains that the first goal of a party is to get into office. To do so, it must win more seats in the House of Commons than any other party. Thus, each party tries to make a general rather than a particular appeal. It attempts to have something for everybody. It tries to have as broad and flexible a point of view as possible, and to attract people from all walks of life, of all religious and racial backgrounds, from all regions and provinces.

In a country as vast and diversified as Canada, this is not an easy task. As we have suggested, the interests of those employed in the Atlantic fisheries, the stock market, the textile industry, the farms, the oil fields and the logging camps are very different. Yet the political party seeks to appeal to all of these voters. As a result, it is often not in the interest of the party to

NATIONAL PARTIES

There are three major parties in national politics. The Liberals and Progressive Conservatives have been in existence since Confederation. They alone have held power in Ottawa. They have dominated the political history of most of the provinces as well. The Liberals and Conservatives, also known as the Grits and the Tories, are broadly based parties. They try to attract support from all occupations, regions, and classes.

The other major party on the national level is the New Democratic Party. It began in 1932-3 as the Co-operative Commonwealth Federation, or the CCF. The CCF was a socialist party that believed that the government should own or control much of our economy. In an attempt to increase its support among farmers, trade unionists, and the middle class, the CCF gradually watered down many of its socialist ideas. Finally, in 1961, it changed its name to the New Democratic Party to try to appeal to non-socialists. The NDP has been an important force in national politics. It has formed the government in Saskatchewan, Manitoba, and British Columbia. More important, however, its leaders have continually prodded the older parties towards policies that are more left-of-centre, and have seen many NDP objectives achieved.

A smaller party, Social Credit, was born during the depression of the 1930s. Social Credit had its home in Alberta, where farmers saw produce rotting in the fields because no one could afford to buy it. The answer to "poverty in the midst of plenty," stated the Social Credit platform, was the use of government credit to provide purchasing power during bad times. The "Socreds" were in power in Alberta from 1935 to 1971, and formed the government in neighbouring British Columbia from 1952 to 1972 and were elected again in 1975. Federally, they elected a handful of members from the west until 1968, when the party was wiped out. The Quebec wing, known as the Ralliement des Créditistes, however, continues to exist as a minor party on the national scene, although in the 1980 election it won no seats.

state its policies too clearly. It may be safer for a party to attack its opponents than to attempt to make its own positions clear.

In defence of politicians, however, it must be said that many of the issues are not clear-cut. Solutions to them are neither simple nor obvious. Moreover, we the voters are often unclear about what we want or how to go about getting what we want. Today most Canadians are in favour of efforts to control pollution, to develop the economy of the country and to improve the standard of living for the disadvantaged. But what happens when discussion turns from the desired goals to the means to achieve them? Agreement ends. How much should governments interfere in our lives? Do we want higher personal

Issues

Two appeals to the people. Cartoonist Arch Dale was hitting out at his favourite target, the Conservative leader R. B. Bennett, in this 1930 election cartoon. Bennett won the election. Ten years later, in the 1940 election, MacNab, the CCF candidate in Kamloops, felt that the issues were straightforward. MacNab ran a poor third, as Mackenzie King and the Liberals swept the country.

taxes? Is pollution control more important than economic development? For the voter as for the party, political decisions involve many "trade-offs." If taxes are not raised, there is no more money to be spent unless the government borrows and goes into debt. If taxes *are* raised, should the money be spent on education, highways, pollution control, helping the poor, or subsidizing athletics? Each decision is a matter of judgement. No one person has a monopoly on truth or wisdom. What is not true is that the government can spend more at the same time as it lowers taxes. And that is often the politician's favourite campaign promise.

It is not only the desire to have the widest possible support that causes similarities among parties. There is also a large measure of agreement among Canadian voters — or American or British for that matter — on many issues. Most of us believe that the government should in some way protect citizens against starvation or malnutrition, sickness or accident. Over the years, public opinion has changed on such matters. Liberals and Progressive Conservatives have become more socialistic. They are willing to move further and faster in providing for the welfare of citizens than they would have twenty or thirty years ago. Socialists, on the other hand, have become more moderate with the achievement of some of their goals.

POLITICAL CHOICE IN CANADA, 1972-1979

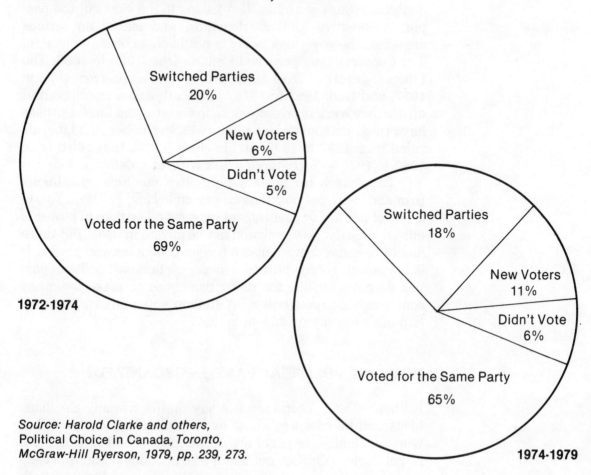

1972-1974

- Switched Parties 20%
- New Voters 6%
- Didn't Vote 5%
- Voted for the Same Party 69%

1974-1979

- Switched Parties 18%
- New Voters 11%
- Didn't Vote 6%
- Voted for the Same Party 65%

Source: Harold Clarke and others,
Political Choice in Canada, *Toronto,*
McGraw-Hill Ryerson, 1979, pp. 239, 273.

They also know that it may not pay politically to be too far in advance of public opinion.

Middle of the Road

To put it another way, in their attempts to win the broadest measure of support from all classes of people and all sections of the country, political parties tend to move toward the middle of the road. That is, they move toward the political centre, avoiding extreme positions on the political "left" or "right." Where possible, they try to force opponents into the ditch on either the left or the right.

Once a party has won solid support in an election through its middle-of-the-road policies, it is hard to remove that party from office. It has many advantages over its rivals. It chooses the time of the next election. It has government jobs and other favours to hand out. And generally it can choose the campaign issues that show it in the best light. Through legislation before the election, the governing party may gain the support of doubtful groups of voters. If it listens to the views of the people, is sensitive to their demands, and makes no serious mistakes, the governing party is not likely to lose an election. The Conservatives governed Canada from 1878 to 1896. The Liberals governed from 1896 to 1911, and again from 1935 to 1957, and from 1963 to 1979, when, after nine months out of office, they were in power again. In Ontario, the Conservatives have ruled without defeat since 1943. In Quebec, the Liberals ruled from 1897 to 1936, and in Nova Scotia, they ruled from 1882 to 1925 — forty-three years without a defeat.

The search for power, then, often conflicts with taking firm and clear-cut positions on principles and policies. Yet, to speak of politics or government in terms other than of power is unreal. Clearly, power should not be an end in itself. But there has to be some compromise between principles and power. It is the task of voting citizens to make certain that political parties do not sacrifice too many principles or make too many compromises to gain power. With their votes, citizens are able to punish when punishment is due.

HOW ARE POLITICAL PARTIES ORGANIZED?

Politicians have been heard to say that in winning elections, ideas and policies are about as helpful as fairy tales. What wins an election is party organization or "the Machine." As Israel Tarte, a Quebec politician who had fought and won elections for thirty years, observed at the dawn of the twentieth century, "Elections are not won with prayers."

Organization

A political party is organized on a number of levels from individual party members up to the party chieftains. At the bottom is the local poll association. Above it are the riding organizations, the regional or provincial associations and finally, the national headquarters. On all levels, except the poll associations, there are women's groups, young people's clubs, study groups and inner circles. Between elections the entire organization generally runs in low gear. But at the first whisper of a new election, the machine moves quickly into high gear.

The members of the organization who come into direct contact with the voters are those belonging to the small local poll associations within each riding. During an election campaign, they knock on doors, identify party supporters, give out literature, put up signs, and try to win the undecided. On election day, they watch at the polling stations. As closing-time ap-

LIBERAL PARTY
PLATFORM

Most national and provincial parties hold large meetings or conventions every year or two. The purpose of such conventions is to keep up party morale, and to bring together the elected members, party officials, and representatives of the "grass roots." At many conventions, the delegates draft the party platform, or policies. As Duncan Macpherson suggests, however, the prime minister and Cabinet may pay little attention to the party platform when determining government policy.

proaches, they telephone those who have not voted and who might vote for their party to remind them of their duty. Sometimes party workers offer transportation or baby-sitting services to get voters to the polls. In other words, they "get out the vote."

Provincial or national headquarters, depending on the election, prepare the over-all campaign program. They arrange for guest speakers on radio and television programs and provide most of the campaign funds or party "war chest."

Finances

National and provincial elections cost the large parties millions of dollars for printing expenses, transportation, radio and television programs, and the renting of offices and halls. A small portion of the money comes from ordinary party members who may give as they would to a club. Much more comes from the wealthy members of the party. These members are asked to contribute large amounts. Most of a party's money has come from people in industry, business, and trade unions. They hope that the party in power will be in sympathy with their point of view. For example, manufacturers are not likely to support a party that favours lower tariffs on imported goods.

The appearance of committee rooms in each riding, the knock on the door by party workers, and signs proclaiming the preference of many residents mark the beginning of an election campaign. The generals are at party headquarters, but the foot soldiers are the local party workers.

Battleford, Saskatchewan, 1911.

Lucille Broadbent canvasses for her husband, 1980.

(Right) Student workers at Carleton University, 1980.

The three major candidates at an all-candidates meeting in the Spadina by-election, 1981.

(Right) Elections can create problems.

Large contributors often give to more than one political party. Sometimes, in an attempt to defeat the government, corporations or individuals have invested heavily in an opposition party, particularly if it seems that that party has a chance of winning the election. On the whole, however, the party in office finds it easier than its opponents to raise money. As a result, it has more money to spend during an election.

Only by freeing the individual politician and the party from their need for funds will the dangers of corruption be reduced. The modern movement for reform began in Quebec, where the record was one of the worst in Canada. Laws passed in 1963 limited the amount each candidate could spend. They also provided that the government would pay the candidates for part of the money they had spent. In 1974, the Trudeau government placed controls on expenses in federal elections. A party was allowed to spend only 30 cents per voter. The candidate could spend no more than one dollar for the first 15 000 voters, 50 cents for the next 10 000, and 25 cents for voters in excess of 25 000. The law also provided for stricter controls on election donations by individuals and corporations, and provided for some free radio and television broadcasting.

Financial Reform

Ontario's Election Finance Reform Act, passed in 1975, took a slightly different approach. It put more emphasis on donations than on expenses. Individuals, trade unions, and corporations could donate a maximum of $4000 a year to a political party, and $4000 during an election campaign. During an election, the amount each party could spend on advertising was limited to 25 cents for every person on the voters list. The act also provided that candidates who received more than 15% of the vote would have some of their expenses paid from public funds.

Other provinces have also passed laws controlling expenses and donations. British Columbia, on the other hand, has been content to prohibit bribing the voters, and has not placed limits on election expenses or donations to political parties. While none of these laws is perfect, the electoral system today is much more honest than it ever was in the past.

HOW IMPORTANT IS THE PARTY LEADER?

Ask people how and why they voted in the last national election. You will find that many, if not most, will say they voted for or against a party leader. Of course, some people vote on the basis of a favourite local candidate or because they agree

Party leaders are chosen by delegates to leadership conventions. Each candidate makes a major speech, and key organizers enlist support. The voting continues until one candidate has a majority. Here, a young Sheila Copps ran a good race against the veteran David Peterson, who won the leadership of the Ontario Liberals in 1982.

or disagree with a particular party policy. But when they vote, many Canadians are really making a decision about which leader they would like to see as prime minister of Canada.

Thus, party leadership is a matter of vital importance. The leader is the party's symbol. He or she must give the appearance of someone who can provide the able and imaginative leadership the country needs. The leader must also manage the Cabinet and the party with enough skill to hold together the many groups and interests that make up the country. Moreover, most of us find many political issues and problems hard to understand. As a result, there is often a temptation to say, "I like or trust A more than B," and hope for the best.

Leadership Qualities

The party leader is the central and most influential figure in Canadian politics. It is important, therefore, to look at those qualities that have contributed to successful leadership in Canada. As we would expect, they are many and varied. Very few people meet all the requirements. Those who do possess these qualities in large measure are likely to remain in office for a long time. This is not to say that every leader must have the same qualities. The jovial, down-to-earth Macdonald, the warm, dignified Laurier, and the aloof, cautious Mackenzie King would seem to have had little in common. Yet beneath the surface they all had, in varying degrees, an unusual ability to sense the common mood, a way with people, a willingness to compromise when necessary, and a nerve as cool as icewater — in all, an acute political sense that is almost impossible to define.

Macdonald, 1867-73, 1878-91

Laurier, 1896-1911

Borden, 1911-1920

King, 1921-6, 1926-30, 1935-48

(Right) St. Laurent, 1948-57

Since 1867 only these prime ministers have been re-elected after one term in office.

(Bottom left) Diefenbaker, 1957-63
(Bottom middle) Pearson, 1963-68
(Bottom right) Trudeau, 1968-79, 1980-

Modern Leaders

Without a gifted leader, a political party is often doomed to remain in opposition, as the national Conservative Party did for more than twenty years after 1935. During that period, it was often said that the Conservative leader was the Liberal Party's best political asset. The Conservative Party changed leaders five times before it found in John Diefenbaker a man who could win an election.

The Liberals had high hopes for Lester Pearson when he took over from Prime Minister Louis St. Laurent after the 1957 election. Pearson had been a brilliant diplomat. But his talents

One view of the election of 1979

in diplomacy were not transferred easily to the public arena or the television screen. The quiet diplomacy of external affairs was not very successful in the rough and tumble of politics. Under Pearson, the Liberals lost the elections of 1958 and 1962. They managed to defeat a tottering Conservative government in 1963, and held onto a slim lead in 1965. However, when Pierre Elliott Trudeau was elected leader of the party in 1968, Liberal fortunes changed overnight. After only a few weeks as prime minister, Trudeau called an election. The dashing bachelor, fluent in two languages, skilled on the diving board and the motorcycle, forthright and sophisticated, inspired some magnetic response in the electorate. What reporters soon called "Trudeaumania" swept the country, and the Liberals coasted to an overwhelming victory.

In office, however, Trudeau seemed less effective than in the campaign. He did not seem to have the answers to the nation's problems. People detected a tone of arrogance in his dealings with the press and Parliament. As a result, many supporters deserted him in the election of 1972. The Liberals narrowly escaped defeat. Learning from this experience, the prime minister entered the campaign of 1974 with much of the confidence and enthusiasm of 1968. Observers gave Trudeau most of the credit for the striking victory of the Liberal Party. By 1979, however, Trudeau had once more become unpopular in many parts of Canada. Again this was due in part to his manner. But it was also due to the fact the Liberal government could not solve the country's serious economic problems. The defeat of Trudeau's party in 1979 by Joe Clark and the Conservatives was regarded generally as a personal defeat. Less than a year later, however, the Liberals were back in office. They were there not because of a sudden upsurge in Trudeau's popularity, but because many voters in some sections of Canada had become convinced that Prime Minister Clark did not have the leadership qualities necessary in a prime minister. By 1982, however, as the country faced the most serious economic crisis since the depression of the 1930s, the popularity of Trudeau and the Liberals sagged again. Public opinion polls in the summer of 1982 indicated that the Liberals would be defeated if there were an election.

Because the party leader is so important, we may sometimes place too much emphasis on the position. A leader without a team can do very little. The cabinet team, made up of the leading members of a political party, is usually a source of strong support for the prime minister. In addition, the prime minister and cabinet team have available their experts in the civil service upon whom they can and must rely. Nevertheless, leadership and direction are essential in a country so diverse and difficult to govern as is Canada. When the country has had weak leadership, it has suffered.

STUDY GUIDE

Getting the Facts

1. Define the following: political party, party policy, party platform, party membership, poll association, riding association, political power, socialist, "motherhood statements."
2. Why are political parties necessary?
3. Why are party platforms often vague and general?
4. What qualities seem to be most important in Canadian political leaders?
5. Why have political parties in Canada tended to remain in power for long periods of time?
6. Draw a chart to show how a political party is organized.
7. (a) What problems have arisen in regard to the funding of political parties?
   (b) How have governments tried to solve these problems?
8. Account for the importance of the party leader.

Using the Facts

1. *Political Spectrum*: Draw a diagram labelled "The Political Spectrum." It should be similar to the colour spectrum. This is a useful way to identify political parties in terms of their policies. The extreme left should be labelled *Radical*, and the extreme right *Reactionary*. Policies that are radical encourage change. Policies that are reactionary are opposed to change. These are the two extremes. On your political spectrum, locate each of the Canadian political parties. Explain why you have placed them as you have.
2. *Debate*: "Resolved that party leadership is more important than party policies."
3. Organize the class into three groups or parties. Have each draw up a party platform designed to attract as many Canadian voters as possible.
4. Why do such a large percentage of Canadian voters remain loyal to the same political party?
5. Does the voting pattern in your family confirm the findings of the pie graphs on page 61?
6. What qualities of political leadership are revealed in the picture opposite of Mr. Pearson that are not suggested in those of the other prime ministers on page 67?

Research Projects

1. *Political Scrapbook*: Gather news clippings outlining actions of each of the federal political parties. Set up a different section for each party. Identify the policy/policies that account for or explain the actions or statements in the clippings selected. On the basis of your evidence, decide whether political parties are concerned mainly with principles or power.

2. (a) Each of the prime ministers on page 67 demonstrated a variety of leadership qualities. Discover the particular qualities that you think best explain the effectiveness of each prime minister.

(b) Which qualities do you think are needed most today?

Chapter 5
HOW DOES PARLIAMENTARY GOVERNMENT WORK?

Who Makes the Laws in Canada?
Law-making
Backbenchers
Opposition
Question Period
The Press

Why Is the Cabinet So Powerful?
Executive Control
Political Power
Collective Responsibility
The Prime Minister

What Does the Cabinet Do?

Do We Need a Senate?
Law-making
Provincial Interests
Senate Reform

Do We Need a Governor General?
Selection of the Prime Minister
Ceremonial Role

Are We Governed by the Civil Service?
Recruitment
Importance
Influence

We have already talked in a very general way about government. We saw that all governments carry on three functions. The legislative function is concerned with making laws. The executive function is concerned with putting the laws into effect on a day-to-day basis, and the judicial function is concerned with upholding the laws. We call the law-making part of government the *legislature*. The branch of government that runs the country on a day-to-day basis is known as the *executive*. The judicial function is carried on by the courts or the *judiciary*. We will discuss the role of the courts later. Here we will concentrate on the operation of the legislature and the executive in the Canadian system of government.

In many countries, including the United States, the legislature and the executive are separate and distinct parts of the government. In the Canadian parliamentary system, which we inherited from Great Britain, the legislature and the executive are united. As the Constitution Act, 1867 (formerly the British North America Act) states:

There shall be one Parliament for Canada, consisting of the Queen, an Upper House styled the Senate and the House of Commons.

In Canada today, the Queen, represented in Canada by the Governor General, is the head of the executive. As we have seen, neither the Queen nor the Governor General can act on their own. Their main task in government is to give formal approval to measures presented to them by the prime minister and Cabinet. The prime minister and cabinet ministers are the real executive in Canada.

Parliament is the legislative branch of government. There are two houses in Parliament. The House of Commons is elected and the Senate is appointed. Since the prime minister and cabinet ministers must have seats in the Commons or the Senate, they are themselves part of the legislature. They may stay in office only as long as they have the support of a majority of members in the Commons. In this way the executive and the legislative branches in the Canadian parliamentary system are united. If a majority of members in the House of Commons refuse to approve a budget or any other important measure introduced by the executive, the prime minister and Cabinet have to resign or call an election. This control of the executive by the legislature is what we mean by *responsible* government. And it is this direct responsibility of the Cabinet (executive) to the Commons (legislature) that provides the key to an understanding of the Canadian parliamentary system.

THE CANADIAN PARLIAMENTARY SYSTEM

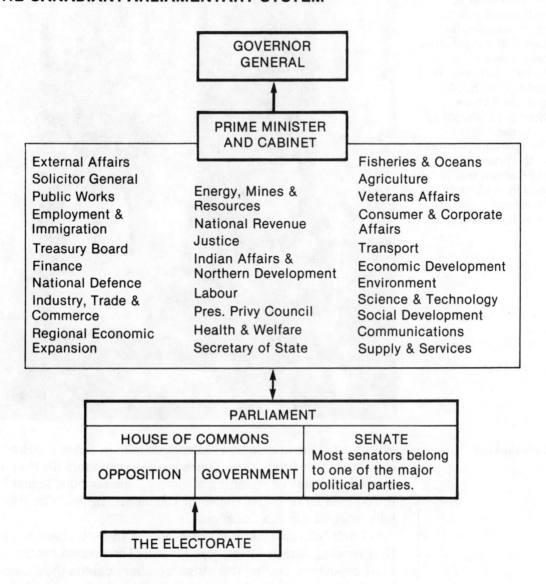

WHO MAKES THE LAWS IN CANADA?

The answer is Parliament. In Canada that means that laws are made by the Queen (Governor General), Senate, and House of Commons. This answer is correct, but it does not explain the process of law-making in Canada. A law is the end product of a very complex process. A law, also known as a statute, begins as a *bill*. A bill becomes a law only after Parliament has approved it.

The statement of government policy, which includes the laws that the government hopes to introduce and pass, is made in the Speech from the Throne when each session of Parliament opens. The speech is written by the prime minister and Cabinet and is read in the Senate Chamber by the Governor General.

Law-making

Members of Parliament may introduce bills in either the House of Commons or the Senate. There is one exception. Bills that involve the raising or spending of money, "money bills," must be introduced first in the House of Commons. In practice, most bills originate in the Commons.

Each bill must have three *readings* in both Houses. The first reading simply introduces the bill. The second reading is most important. During this stage members debate the general principles of the bill, the ideas and convictions on which it is based. Then they may examine the details of the bill. Frequently this is done in the "committee of the whole House." This is a procedure in which the formal rules of debate are relaxed. The bill might then go to a smaller committee of members, called a *standing committee*. These committees often call experts from outside Parliament to give their views. During the second reading there may be amendments made to the bill if they do not affect its general objectives. Finally, the bill receives third reading in the Commons. After that it goes to the Senate. When the Senate approves the bill, it then goes to the Governor General for assent. With the Governor General's signature the bill becomes a law.

But who decides what laws there should be? And how do proposals for such laws reach the House of Commons and the Senate? And how do they pass? Answers to these questions throw much more light on how government actually works than can a mechanical description of how a bill becomes a law. The chart on page 78 answers these questions and *explains* the process using a specific example.

It is easy to see that the Cabinet plays the most important role in the law-making process in Parliament. Indeed, some critics of the parliamentary system say that when the ruling party has a majority, the House of Commons is little more than a rubber stamp for Cabinet decisions. There is some justification for this criticism. But it is a mistake to think that the role of the Commons is simply to pass or defeat the bills introduced by the Cabinet. The Commons plays a vital part in our system of government. It is in the House that our elected representatives examine in public the actions of our government. The record and press coverage of these public debates makes it possible for the voters, too, to play an important part in the governmental process.

Backbenchers

As the key actors on the parliamentary stage, the cabinet ministers must convince the other members of their party in the Commons that the policies proposed by Cabinet are the right ones. The members of the governing party who are not in the Cabinet are called backbenchers because their seats in the House are behind those of the ministers. Naturally, the backbenchers want to be able to support government or Cabinet policies. They do not want to see their party defeated. On the other hand, they know very well the opinions of the people who elected them and they do not want the government to adopt policies that go against such views. As we have seen, one of the ways the public can reach the decision-makers is through their elected representatives. The elected members make the public's views known in the party *caucus*, meetings of all the party members in the Commons and Senate, usually held every week. They also have opportunities to discuss policies and problems with the ministers concerned. Sometimes, backbenchers are unable to agree with a government proposal and will vote against their own leaders. If their disagreement is strong and basic, they may even resign from the party.

Opposition

The opposition parties also play a vital role in the House of Commons. During its debates, they examine and criticize government policies. The leader of the political party with the sec-

PASSING A BILL

1. THE ENVIRONMENT

Among the people and the oil and gas industry — the *political environment* — there is a growing conviction that somehow Canada must become self-sufficient in energy.

2. DEMANDS

This conviction leads to *demands* for changes in the country's energy policy to encourage new exploration for oil and gas. These demands reach the government through the press, the politicians and the industry's pressure group.

3. DECISIONS

(a) The Cabinet discusses the problem and agrees that they must *respond*. The prime minister instructs the minister of energy to prepare recommendations.

(b) The minister of energy meets with senior advisers in the civil service and asks them to draft the required recommendations. The minister may also discuss the problem with representatives of industry.

(c) When the recommendations have been prepared, the minister brings them to the Cabinet. If the Cabinet approves them, the minister tells the civil servants to prepare a detailed bill. (At this stage the prime minister or the minister may announce that the government is planning a new policy.)

4. RESPONSE

The bill reaches the Commons and Senate. Opposition members will criticize it while government members defend it. While the tactics of each party are determined by the leaders, the day-to-day work is organized by the party *whips*, who make sure their members are all in the House for important votes. When the bill passes, the Governor General gives it "Royal Assent." Canada has a new energy law and a new energy policy. The environment is changed.

(d) Before bringing the bill to the House of Commons, the minister will inform the members of the government party in the Commons and Senate of the new proposal. The minister will make this presentation at the party *caucus* or meeting of party members. There is usually a caucus every week when Parliament is in session. At caucus, the minister will explain the policy, answer questions and try to persuade those who are opposed. The minister's main goal is to make sure that all members of the party understand the party's official position on the bill and will support it during the debate.

ond largest number of seats in the House is called the Leader of the Opposition. He or she and the leaders of the other opposition parties try to put the government on the defensive, to make it appear ineffective. They have many opportunities to do so, for the rules of the Commons permit lengthy debate on every government bill. Opposition members are also included in standing committees. They are thus in a position to look closely at the smallest detail of a bill. As a result, the government may change features of a bill and improve it. But the major objective of the opposition parties is not to help the government work better. Their main concern is to convince the public that they and not the government should be running the country.

The prime minister replies to his critics during question period. The questions are often really an attack on the government. Question period is one time when the leaders of the opposition parties and the prime minister and members of the Cabinet try to be in the House.

Question Period

To help in this objective, the opposition parties make great use of the hour known as *question period*. This period takes place every afternoon when the House meets. During question period the Opposition controls what goes on in the Commons. They may ask questions of the prime minister and cabinet ministers on almost any topic they wish. Often they try to trap ministers into making statements that have not been thought out carefully. They demand to know whether a decision has been made or not. As often as possible, the Opposition points out differences between what a cabinet minister has said and what the prime minister has said on the same subject. Sometimes, the opposition parties have information which suggests that the government is not being completely straightforward in what it says. Such information may be the result of their own research. Sometimes it is supplied secretly by civil servants or others who believe that the government should be exposed.

The probing that takes place during question period supplies much of the material we read in newspapers or watch on television. Certainly this hour in the afternoon is the most interesting and often the most important period of the Commons' debates. No good parliamentary reporter would miss the question period, although the press gallery may empty shortly after it is finished.

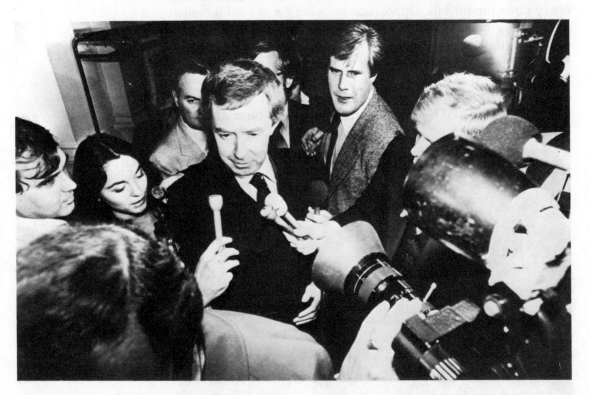

The Press

The scrum: radio, television, and newspaper reporters patrol the corridors of the Commons to catch party leaders or cabinet ministers as they emerge from a debate, or, in this case, a meeting of the party caucus. It does resemble a scrimmage in rugger — thus the word scrum.

The press — newspapers, radio and television — provides our window on Parliament. When the Opposition attacks the government, it is really speaking to us through the press. As the press reports on the battle of words taking place on the floor of the House below, it gives us the information we need to decide how well our representatives are serving us. The way in which the press reports the battle is also important, for it may shape our opinions and, thus, help to decide the winners and losers. We also form judgements on the quality of our representatives as we watch live telecasts of their performances or selected snippets on TV news programs.

Reports in the press may not always be accurate or fair. But it is difficult to see how our democracy could work without the press. When the government has a large majority in the Commons, it is not likely to lose the parliamentary battle. But the work of the opposition parties and the press may so influence the Canadian people that the government will lose the war during the next election.

WHY IS THE CABINET SO POWERFUL?

So important is the Cabinet in the government of Canada that we often use the words cabinet and government as if they were the same. How often we hear the words, the Trudeau government or the Clark government or the Lougheed government or the Davis government! Each occasion underlines the powerful position of the party leader and the appointed ministers of the Cabinet.

The Cabinet is important first of all because it is the real executive of the country. As a rule it controls a majority in the legislature. The Cabinet decides what policies the government will follow. It decides whether the country will be at peace or war, whether to raise or lower taxes, whether to improve airports or increase old-age pensions. In addition to its responsibility for almost all legislation, the Cabinet also has the power to make laws in the form of Orders in Council. These orders, which must formally be approved by the Governor General, must fall within a power given to the government by a law passed by Parliament. But in many cases the law is very general, and gives the Cabinet very wide powers to issue rules and regulations in the form of Orders in Council.

Executive Control

A second reason for the Cabinet's power is that the prime minister and cabinet ministers are the leading members of the party in power. The prime minister *is* prime minister because he or she is the leader of the victorious political party. The prime minister chooses members of the Cabinet from among

Political Power

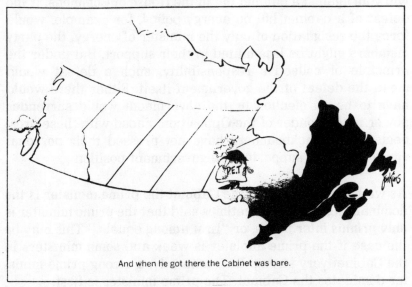

And when he got there the Cabinet was bare.

In the election of 1980, no Liberals were elected in the three western provinces. Only two were elected from Manitoba. As a result, Prime Minister Trudeau appointed members of the Senate from Saskatchewan, Alberta, and British Columbia to his Cabinet.

the leading members of the party. Usually there is at least one member from every province. If no party member is elected from a province, the prime minister is likely to choose someone in the Senate from that province to represent the province in the Cabinet. As a general rule, the larger the province, the more members it will have in the Cabinet.

In addition to provincial representation, the prime minister also tries to appoint as ministers people who represent important cultural, religious and economic interests. In the past twenty years there have usually been women in the Cabinet and members of minority groups. The Cabinet, then, represents the diversity in the country and in the party. Within the party, the cabinet team led by the prime minister is very powerful indeed. Very few backbenchers in the caucus would oppose the party leadership. And for anyone who had ambitions to become a cabinet minister, it might be a risky course to take a stand against the prime minister.

Collective Responsibility

A third reason for the power of the prime minister and Cabinet is because they follow the principle of what is called *collective responsibility*. This means that cabinet ministers in private may disagree on what is the best policy to follow. Once the Cabinet makes its decision, however, every minister must support that decision and take responsibility for it. If a cabinet minister cannot support a decision, the only alternative is to resign from the Cabinet.

Everyone in the party understands the importance of collective responsibility. Backbenchers know that it is difficult to change any policy or decision that has the support of a united Cabinet. And it is highly unlikely that members of the party will vote against a cabinet bill in the House of Commons. If the defeat of a cabinet bill on energy policy, for example, would force the resignation of only the minister of energy, the party members might be less united in their support. But under the principle of collective responsibility, such a defeat would mean the defeat of the government itself. Either there would have to be an election or the government would surrender power to the Leader of the Opposition. Faced with these prospects, many backbenchers have not pressed their personal views and have supported the government position.

The Prime Minister

As we have seen, within the Cabinet the prime minister is the dominant figure. It is sometimes said that the prime minister is only *primus inter pares*, or "first among equals." This may be the case if the prime minister is weak and some ministers in the Cabinet very strong. But, generally, a strong prime minister dominates the Cabinet. The prime minister *is* first.

There are several reasons for this dominance. The prime minister is the leader of the party. Many members of the Cabinet and the Commons may have been elected because the party leader was strong and popular. The prime minister also chooses personally all members of the Cabinet and may dismiss them or give them more attractive positions. Usually the prime minister is able to control even the most powerful of ministers. However, strong ministers occasionally have tried to challenge the prime minister. The prime minister may bow to the challenge and change his or her mind. But, if this does not happen and the Cabinet supports the prime minister, the minister must accept defeat or resign. During the first ten years of Prime Minister Trudeau's term, several ministers did resign openly on questions of policy. They soon found themselves in the political shadows. Other ministers seemed to tire of the prime minister's leadership and retired from politics. Their actions had little effect on the prime minister's position in the Cabinet.

The prime minister is so powerful, in fact, that only once in Canadian history has a cabinet revolt forced the prime minister to quit and let someone else take over. When this happened, in 1896, there were seven strong cabinet ministers lined up against a very weak and old prime minister. In 1963, Prime Minister Diefenbaker was able to survive the resignation of one strong minister and a revolt of several others. However, the Canadian people did not support him and defeated his government in the 1963 election.

WHAT DOES THE CABINET DO?

The prime minister and Cabinet decide what policies the country will follow. Platforms of their political party may guide them. Demands from the people, from pressure groups and from the press may influence them. But in the end the Cabinet must make the decisions and hope that Parliament and the people will support them.

Since Confederation, the functions of government have increased greatly. In 1867 there were only eleven cabinet ministers. Today there are more than thirty. Each member of the Cabinet is usually in charge of a ministry or government department. (See chart on page 75.) However, there are about a dozen Ministers of State responsible for such areas as Fitness, Small Business and Tourism, Multiculturalism and International Trade. They are also members of the Cabinet, but they do not head independent government departments. The government leader in the Senate is also a member of the Cabinet.

Cabinet ministers who head up departments are responsible for the policies of those departments. Before a policy can be put into operation, it must receive the approval of the whole Cabinet. The process is seldom easy, for there is a limited amount of money to spend on all of the programs the various ministers want to put into effect. Approval for the program of one department may mean that another has to give up its program.

Individual ministers must answer in the House of Commons for the work of their departments. This task often presents difficulties, for ministers do not have to be expert in the area of their responsibility. For example, the minister of transportation may have had no training in this field. There have been ministers of agriculture who have not farmed, and ministers of defence who have not had military experience. However, all ministers have staffs of experts in their departments. These experts advise them how to justify department spending or to present bills dealing with the department. However well or badly the ministers perform in Parliament, they know that they have the support of their colleagues in the Cabinet and party. An attack on one minister is an attack on all.

The Cabinet not only carries out executive and legislative functions, it also acts as a political body. For it is impossible to separate the work of government and the life of a political party. The Cabinet decides what will be best for the country, but it is also concerned with what will be good for their party. In this sense, the Cabinet also fulfills a role as an important means of communication between the people and their government.

"Come on, fellows, it was just a quip...all I said was Ottawa intends
to be absolutely brutal on wasteful spending..."

Control of government spending is one of the most important issues in Canada. In the Commons, government spending is examined in standing committees. According to Geoffrey Stevens, in The Globe and Mail, June 21, 1982, the system is a "disaster. MPs have neither the time nor the interest to do the homework to probe details of complicated expenditure programs." Since 1969, the MPs have slashed a total of $1000 from $500 billion in government spending!

Government spending is examined after the fact by the Auditor General, who is appointed by the government, but can be dismissed only by Parliament. Recent Auditors General have been very critical of waste in government spending. As the Auditor General warned in 1976: "Parliament — and indeed the Government — has lost or is close to losing effective control of the public purse."

DO WE NEED A SENATE?

So far we have said little about the Senate, the second chamber in the legislature. The Upper House, as it is known, is made up of one hundred and four men and women. Senators are not elected like members of the Commons, but are appointed by the Governor General on the recommendation of the prime minister. To be a senator, one must be thirty years old and have property worth $4000. Senators used to remain in office for life, but since 1965, they must retire at age seventy-five.

Law-making

The Senate was designed to share the function of law-making with the House of Commons. All bills have to pass in the Senate as well as the Commons. But the Fathers of Confederation knew when they created the Senate that it would never be as important as the Commons whose members were elected by the people. The Fathers believed, however, that a body made up of people of wealth — in 1867, $4000 was a considerable sum — would act as a useful check on what Sir John A. Macdonald described as "hasty or ill-considered legislation" that the Commons might pass. But Macdonald added that the appointed Senate "will never set itself in opposition against the deliberate and understood wishes of the people."

In practice, the Senate has not been very important as a check on the Commons. Unlike the American Senate, it is not elected. The Canadian Senate speaks for no one but itself. Although it can and has refused to pass bills introduced by the Cabinet, this does not mean that the government must resign as would a similar defeat in the Commons. The Cabinet may agree to change the bill, but if it does not, the Senate usually gives way. The government no longer regards the Senate as very important. The Leader of the Government in the Senate is usually the only cabinet minister to sit in the Senate. (However, when the Liberals failed to elect any members from the three western provinces in 1980, Prime Minister Trudeau selected cabinet ministers from the Senate to represent western Canada.) The press shares the view that the Senate is not important. As a result, it seldom reports Senate debates.

Provincial Interests

The Fathers also believed that the Senate should represent provincial interests in Parliament. They gave equal representation of twenty-four members each to Ontario, Quebec, and the Atlantic provinces. They extended the principle as the other provinces came into federation. Today there are twenty-four members each from Ontario and Quebec, ten from Nova Scotia and from New Brunswick, four from Prince Edward Island, six from each of the other provinces, and one from each of the Yukon and the Northwest Territories.

Just as the Senate has not served as much of a check on

WHEN HEADS ROLL IN GOVERNMENT, THEY TEND TO ROLL UPHILL

the Commons, neither has it been an effective guardian of provincial or regional interests. Although senators must be appointed on the basis of provincial quotas, they are appointed by the prime minister, not the provincial governments. Often their appointments are rewards for party services. As a result, they owe their loyalty to the prime minister and to the party, not the provinces.

Since the Senate does not serve the purposes for which it was set up, many Canadians are convinced that we do not need it. Many politicians while in Opposition have suggested that the Senate be abolished. Once in power, however, they find the Senate useful for paying political debts. On the whole, there has never been a strong movement to do away with the Senate, perhaps because the Canadian people care very little about it.

Most of the discussion about the Senate has centred on ways to improve it. A frequent suggestion is that appointments to the Senate should honour distinguished Canadians — scientists, journalists, artists, and writers, soldiers and teachers. There

Senate Reform

have been some recent appointments of this kind. But would we expect such people to act as a check on the House of Commons or to serve as representatives of the provinces or regions?

There have been suggestions that the Senate should become a body that truly represents the provinces. During the debate that led to the new Canadian constitution, many of the provinces urged that provincial governments appoint the senators. They also urged that the Senate should have a special role to play in any case in which laws would affect the provinces. Some observers believed that such proposals had merit. Others thought that the country did not need another area in which the central government and the provinces would come into conflict.

Sooner or later Canadians will have to reach a decision about the Senate. Few people today seem convinced that we need it. Unless a changed Senate has a useful role to play, it will probably disappear.

DO WE NEED A GOVERNOR GENERAL?

Before Canada became an independent nation, the British government appointed the Governor General. His main duty was to keep an eye on Britain's colony. Today, the Canadian government appoints the Governor General. There is no connection with the British government. We have seen that the system of responsible government means that the Governor General, like the Queen in Great Britain, acts only on the advice of the prime minister and the Cabinet. For this reason some Canadians believe that the Governor General is merely a rubber stamp for the Cabinet. The country, they argue, has no need for such "rubber stamps" in government and the office should be abolished. Should it? Does the Governor General have any important functions or powers?

Selection of the Prime Minister

What would happen tomorrow if the prime minister were to die? There would then be no government of Canada. In such a circumstance, the Governor General would meet immediately with the deputy prime minister who in turn would meet with members of the Cabinet and other leading members of the party in power. If they could agree on a temporary leader, the Governor General would ask that person to form a new government. If they could not agree, the Governor General would have to choose someone to become prime minister and to form a Cabinet so that the government could be carried on. Under

THE CANADIANIZATION OF THE GOVERNOR GENERAL

The Governor General was originally not only the representative of the Crown but also an official responsible to the British government. But in 1926, when Canada's independence was for all practical purposes recognized, the Governor General no longer represented the British government. Thereafter, the Governor General was appointed by the monarch on the advice of the Canadian government. Not until 1952, however, did the Canadian government recommend a Canadian, Vincent Massey, for the position.

(Top) Lord Aberdeen and staff, 1894. (Middle) Vincent Massey arrives to open Parliament in 1958. (Bottom) Governor General Schreyer awards medals to Boy Scouts in 1979.

these circumstances, then, the Governor General might have an important function to carry out. But even in this case, the Governor General's actual power would be limited because a newly appointed prime minister would have to have the support of the House of Commons in order to carry on the government.

A Governor General might also have to decide which party had the right to form a government. For example, what would happen if the next election returned ninety-four members from each of three parties? No party would have a majority. If the prime minister resigned, who would be asked to become prime minister? The person who was Leader of the Opposition before the election? The leader of the party that won the largest number of votes in the election? The person suggested by the retiring prime minister as best able to win the support of the other parties? Or what would happen if the prime minister decided to try to continue governing but was defeated immediately in the House of Commons? Should there be another election, or should the prime minister resign and let someone else try to form a government? These questions suggest that situations might arise which would require the Governor General to make a decision in order that the country's business could be carried on.

Ceremonial Role

If such unlikely developments were the only reasons for having a Governor General, we might conclude that there was little real need to keep the office. But the Governor General performs other duties. The Governor General entertains important foreign visitors and honours distinguished Canadians, cuts the ribbons to open hospitals and art galleries, and lends support to a great many worthy causes and events. Canadians like such ceremonies and, at times, they are better carried out by someone who is above the hurly-burly of politics. And in this way, the prime minister is free to concentrate on running the country.

Although it is hard to measure, probably the most important role of the office of Governor General is that it serves as a reminder of our past. The opening of every session of Parliament is crammed with history, from the arrival of the Governor General's carriage before the Parliament Buildings, to the procession to the Senate Chamber, to the invitation to the Commons to stand at the bar of the door to the Senate and listen to the Speech from the Throne, read by the Governor General. Such ceremonies bring to what was a lumber town on the Ottawa River a reminder of the majesty and drama of a thousand years of struggle for the free institutions we enjoy today.

ARE WE GOVERNED BY THE CIVIL SERVICE?

One of the most important parts of our system of government is the civil service. It is made up of all those people who serve or work for the government. Included in its ranks are men and women from every walk of life and from almost every imaginable occupation. There are clerks and typists, painters and poets, construction workers, teachers, post-office workers, doctors and an army of lawyers and scientists. The most noteworthy single fact about the civil service is that it is large. Over one million Canadians — one out of every ten working Canadians — work for governments at one level or another.

Senior members of the civil service, often called mandarins, after the wise men who once advised the rulers of China, must share in much of the credit and the blame for government policies. There are many outside Ottawa who do not have a very high opinion of their wisdom — or that of their masters.

Recruitment

At one time in Canada it was common practice for a victorious political party to appoint its "friends," those people who had worked for or supported the party, to posts in the civil service. This practice was known as the "spoils system," from the phrase "to the victors belong the spoils." Today, few Canadians believe that the spoils system is a satisfactory way to recruit the people who will do some of the country's most important work. Most of us are convinced that the civil service should be independent of politics and that it should contain the best people possible. Thus, we accept the principle that entrance to the civil service should be based on clearly established standards, and that promotion should be based on merit only. Although the spoils system is certainly not dead in Canada, the general use of competitive entrance examinations and promotion on worth have produced a very good civil service.

Importance

It is no exaggeration to say that without the civil service our government could not function for even a short period of time. Civil servants are important because they perform the multitude of routine tasks essential in any large corporation. They are also absolutely vital because they provide the expertise in such specialized areas as energy, diplomacy and finance. Highly educated people, who have spent years mastering the details of particular subjects, fill most of the higher positions in every department of the service. For the most part, they stay in these positions regardless of what political party is in power. These civil servants thus provide a desirable continuity in government services.

Cabinet ministers have beliefs and ideas. But they seldom have a deep and detailed knowledge of the affairs of the departments they head. They must depend on the assistance and advice given by their experts, the senior permanent public servants. So great is this dependence that people often claim that we are really governed by our civil servants.

There is some truth in the statement. Government has become so complex and difficult to understand that we simply cannot get along without highly skilled experts. This situation raises problems. One hundred years ago citizens who seriously studied public affairs could understand the issues facing the country and reach intelligent conclusions about them. Today, this is often not the case. There are difficult economic, financial and social questions that seem to defy solution by anyone. Even the experts cannot agree on whether there should be more or less money in circulation or whether unemployment is less damaging than inflation in the long run. When intelligent citizens find that they cannot understand the issues, there is little they can do but side with their favourite party, leader, or newspaper. Such a situation is unhealthy, for elections usually involve difficult and complex problems. And elections do not make much sense if the voters do not really understand the issues involved.

Influence

It is true that the experts in the civil service act only as advisers to the cabinet ministers in charge of departments. But when civil servants work closely with cabinet ministers for a number of years, they often come to have a great deal of influence and even control over the affairs of departments of government. As a result, new ministers representing a different political party, may feel that they cannot rely on the loyalty of their advisers. The situation may become particularly awkward when a new minister asks a civil servant to carry out a policy that is in conflict with one that that civil servant has helped to form. Sometimes cabinet ministers are pledged to support policies that the experts think are ill-advised or impossible to carry out. If there is such a great difference of opinion between a cabinet minister and a senior civil servant that the expert is not willing to carry out the minister's policy, the civil servant will resign.

On the whole, Canada's civil servants have earned their reputation as a reasonably impartial, able, and honest group of administrators. As their importance and influence continue to grow with the increase in government activities, it is important to ensure that the quality of the civil service remains high.

STUDY GUIDE

Getting the Facts

1. Define each of the following: legislature, executive, responsible government, bill, law, Committee of the Whole House, standing committee, amendment, caucus, rubber stamp, backbencher, question period, minister, collective responsibility, "primus inter pares," spoils system.
2. Why is the House of Commons the dominant part of our parliamentary system?
3. What are money bills?
4. What is the role of each of the following: the electorate, a member of Parliament, the House of Commons, the Senate, the Governor General, the majority party, the official Opposition, the prime minister, the Cabinet, cabinet ministers, the civil service.

Using the Facts

1. If you were prime minister of Canada, how would you choose members of your Cabinet? On what bases would you assign them to ministries? How would you use the party caucus to strengthen your position?
2. You belong to a political party in your riding and must select a candidate for the next election. What qualifications would you like to see in the person selected?
3. Should members of Parliament act according to the wishes of the majority in their constituency? Should they follow their own convictions? Under what circumstances should backbenchers vote against their own political party? What might be the consequences?

Research Projects

1. *The American System of Checks and Balances.* The American and Canadian systems of government have much in common. Both are democratic. Both have representative government and political parties. Both live under the rule of law. However, there are many differences between the two systems.

   The president of the United States is voted for separately by the people. The president cannot be a member of Congress, or the legislative branch. Indeed, the president often belongs to a different party than that which controls the Senate or the House of Representatives — the two houses in the Congress. The Americans believe that the executive and legislative functions of government should be separate. For example, Congress may ignore the president's recommendations. The president may in turn veto any bill passed by Congress. There must be a two thirds vote of both the Senate and the House of Representatives to overcome a presidential veto.

Another striking difference between the Canadian and American systems is the method of making Cabinet appointments. The president may appoint to his or her Cabinet any American citizen he/she thinks is qualified. These ministers are responsible only to the president. They may not sit in Congress. They are not elected. However, the Senate must approve each Cabinet appointment.

The relationship between the executive and legislative branches of government in the American system is known as "checks and balances," or the separation of powers. It is strikingly different from the Canadian system of responsible government. Each system has advantages and disadvantages.

Using the information here as a basis for research, write an essay discussing

(a) which system is more democratic,

(b) which system is more efficient,

(c) which is more powerful, the prime minister or the president.

In your conclusion, explain the reasons for your preference for either the Canadian or the American system.

2. *Passing a Private Member's Bill*

When the House of Commons is in session, the manner in which the time is used is tightly organized. As might be expected, most of the time is spent debating legislation proposed by the government. Some time, however, is set aside for the debate of bills introduced by private members. Such bills do not have much chance of becoming law since the time allotted to discuss them often runs out before debate is complete.

You are the MP for a large industrial constituency. Some of your constituents have persuaded you to introduce a Private Member's Bill that will severely restrict sulphur emissions and thereby reduce the *acid rain* that is harming the Canadian environment. How would you arrange to get your bill introduced in the House of Commons? How would you organize support for the bill? How would you deal with arguments from affected industries?

Chapter 6
SHOULD WE RELY ON THE MASS MEDIA?

How Healthy Is Our Press?
Partisanship

Who Owns the Press?
Big Business
Editorial Freedom
Increasing Concentration
The Kent Report
One-newspaper Towns
Multi-media Ownership
Mixing Oil and Newsprint

Do Advertisers Influence the Press?
Advertising and Quality
Advertising and Press Freedom

How Has the Government Responded?
Proposed Press Law

**The Canadian Broadcasting Corporation:
How Well Does It Perform?**
Responsibility to Parliament

Why include the *mass media* in a study of government? What do newspapers, radio and television have to do with government and politics? The answer is that we depend almost completely on the mass media — often simply called *the press* — for our information about the political world around us. We seldom visit Parliament or the provincial legislatures. We do not have many chances to question our representatives in government or other politicians. Nor do we often have the time or the desire to read long speeches and reports on even the most important subjects.

The simple truth is that most of our information is second-hand. The people who own, manage, and write for the mass media choose our information for us. We may not always believe what we read, see, or hear. But there can be no doubt that the mass media has a great influence on the way we look at the world. In modern society, the mass media has enormous power. As Eugene Hallman, who has worked for many years in the Canadian media, wrote:

Publishers are dealing in power, the power to disclose information or deny disclosure, to provide a free range of opinion, or to provide some of it; to cool public opinion or to heat it up. . . . The front page and the editorial page announce what and who are important and why they are.

In dictatorships, the government either controls the mass media or makes it an actual part of the government. Those who rule in a dictatorship or a country that allows only one party know that a free press is one of the greatest enemies of tyrants and oppressors. A free press and an unfree society cannot exist together.

Canadians believe that a free press is essential in a democracy. The press should give citizens honest information so that they can reach sound conclusions. It should also act as a watchdog to make sure that governments "behave" by acting in the public interest. Democracy in the modern world has never existed without a free press. And a free press has never existed in an undemocratic society. For these reasons, we must be deeply concerned about the health and freedom of our mass media.

HOW HEALTHY IS OUR PRESS?

Although Canadian journalism and broadcasting is generally of good quality, some people believe that it may be too partisan. To be *partisan* is to support strongly a party or cause,

HOW CANADIANS VIEW THE MASS MEDIA

NEWSPAPERS   RADIO   TELEVISION

Canadians were asked:
Which of the three information media, newspapers, radio or TV . . .

Keeps you up-to-date

27%	27%	52%

Is most fair and unbiased

29%	32%	53%

Is most influential

23%	14%	67%

Is most essential to Canada

35%	24%	52%

Is most essential to your community

53%	25%	27%

Is most essential to you personally

39%	28%	39%

Presents widest range of opinions

44%	18%	43%

Is most believable

34%	28%	54%

Source: Royal Commission on Newspapers, *Ministry of Supply and Services Canada, 1981, p. 35*

perhaps without questioning, or without seeing more than one side of an issue. Other words often used to mean the same thing are *biased* or *prejudiced*. Many of us are partisan on some matters. Sometimes, we refuse even to listen to arguments that support a point of view different from our own. The people who own and produce newspapers and radio and television programs are very much like the rest of us. The important question is whether they are partisan when they decide what we shall read, hear, and view.

Partisanship

Until quite recently, perhaps three decades ago, most newspapers were partisan. They were clearly Conservative or Liberal. They felt that one of their main functions was to help political parties to gain power or to work for their defeat. In short, they tried to make or unmake governments.

Once in peacetime, a government in Canada did attempt to control the press. In 1937, angered by criticism of his Social Credit government, Premier Aberhart of Alberta passed The Accurate News and Information Bill which limited press freedom. The Toronto Globe and Mail thundered that there was nothing "in the way of press control, outside the Fascist and Communist countries, that is comparable with it in suppression of freedom of personal liberty." The bill never became law because the Lieutenant Governor did not assent to it and the Supreme Court ruled that the province did not have the power to pass it.

Today, there are few newspapers and no radio or television stations that are clearly tied to a political party. However, the political *sympathies* of many newspapers are easily seen. During election campaigns, newspapers often will state in editorials the party they favour. No one questions their right to express such opinions on the editorial page. (We might question their influence, however. In the 1974 federal election, all three Toronto newspapers supported the Conservative Party, but the Liberals won most of the Toronto seats!)

We are not upset by partisanship as long as it appears only in editorials or in signed columns, which everyone clearly knows to be the personal opinion of the writer. It is a matter of concern when it creeps into the coverage and presentation of the news.

It is not always easy to detect partisanship in news coverage. The use of headlines, the general tone of a news article and its location in the newspaper or radio or television report, the kind of pictures and cartoons used, the choice of words and tone of voice may all be intended to influence a reader or viewer. After a detailed study of the media, Professor Fred Fletcher, a Canadian journalist and political scientist, observed in 1981:

Researchers are agreed . . . that the news media, through their selection and presentation of news, can reinforce voting decisions, help to form images of leaders and parties, and influence the selection of issues and the tone of the campaign, all in ways that may work to the advantage of one party or the other.

Everyone agrees that the task of presenting the news is difficult. Every day, reporters and editors must choose from great masses of material what to include in the paper, report on the radio, or show on the screen. They must also decide how to present the material. They constantly ask such questions as: "Is it really news? Is it important news? Is it correct? Will it interest people? Will it offend or anger?" Each answer is in many ways a personal decision. It is difficult to be completely free of bias. What matters is that the media should try very hard to give the public fair and honest coverage of the news.

The mass media in Canada is reasonably good. But we must always be aware of the fact that someone is usually standing between the news and us. As we have said, we get most of our information about politics and government second-hand.

"Get moving. Someone has to go and you're it!"

—Carless, Solidarity Canada, United Auto Workers

Cartoons, which we use so frequently in this book, are the personal editorial statements of the artist. In most cases, the editorial statement in the cartoon is discussed by the editor of the paper and his or her staff. The cartoons appear on the editorial pages of newspapers to indicate that they are personal statements of opinion. What editorial statement is being made in these cartoons by John Collins in the Montreal Gazette, (bottom right) January 7, 1981, Uluschak in the Edmonton Journal (bottom left) January 15, 1981, and Carless, Solidarity Canada, United Auto Workers, 1976 (top)?

NEW YEAR'S RESOLUTION

Some Canadians argue that in one way the mass media is completely partisan, because it tends to show only one side of the political scene. In the 1980 federal election, for example, 20% of Canadians voted for the NDP. In Ontario, 30% of the people regularly support the NDP. British Columbia, Manitoba, and Saskatchewan have each had NDP governments. Yet nowhere in Canada is there a newspaper that regularly supports NDP policies or urges its readers to elect a left-wing government. Why not? Many students of the media claim that the answer is to be found by looking at who owns the press.

WHO OWNS THE PRESS?

The table on page 104 shows who owns the daily press in Canada.

Big Business

Clearly, with the exception of a few small local stations and community newspapers, the media today is "big business." Millions of dollars are needed to buy and run a daily newspaper or a major television station. The rewards are also high. The daily newspapers have incomes of more than $1.2 billion a year. In 1980, the media — newspapers, radio and television — sold $2.1 billion of advertising. The people who own the press are business people just like those who own and control other industrial, commercial, and financial enterprises. All run their businesses for the same basic purpose — to make a profit. This fact raises questions about the freedom and fairness of the press.

Some media owners claim that they give their editors and producers a free hand in deciding what to put in their papers or to cover in their news programs. And it may be true that the owners do not often interfere directly in the day-to-day running of a paper, radio, or television station. But Beland Honderich, publisher of the Toronto *Star*, admitted that the owners do have great influence:

Editorial Freedom

Even if this control is not exercised directly, it is exercised indirectly through budget controls and the selection of publishers and editors. For the same reason that independent publishers tend to hire people that reflect their opinions, the owners of group newspapers select people whose opinions do not vary greatly from their own.

Sometimes newspaper owners have interfered directly. During the Quebec referendum of 1980, for example, Paul Desmarais (Gesca) would not let any of his newspapers support the pro-independence side. Jacques Francoeur, owner of *Le Soleil*, wanted to print editorials on each side of the question. When he could find no one to write an editorial opposing independence, he decided that there would be no editorials!

Before the outbreak of the First World War in 1914, there were 138 newspapers and 138 newspaper owners in Canada. Today there are 111 newspapers and 38 owners. Of even greater interest is the fact that four companies produce four out of every five newspapers read in English-speaking Canada. In Quebec, about 90% of the population read papers produced by only three owners.

Increasing Concentration

This concentration of ownership of the press in Canada has long been a matter of concern. The concern became alarm in 1980. In that year the Thomson chain bought all the newspapers owned by FP Publications which had had 22% of English-language circulation. It was not only the size of the deal that worried Canadians. The sale brought within the Thomson group some of Canada's oldest and best newspapers, including

OWNERSHIP OF DAILY NEWSPAPERS IN CANADA, 1982

Owner	No.*	Weekly Circulation (000 000s)	% of National Circulation	Weeklies and Magazines	Radio-TV	Other business**
Southam	14	8.7	27	Yes	Yes	No
Thomson	38	6.7	21	Yes	No	Yes
Sun (Maclean Hunter)	3	2.2	7	Yes	Yes	No
Irving	3	.8	2.5	No	Yes	Yes
Armadale	2	.7	2.2	No	Yes	Yes
Sterling	11	.3	.9	Yes	Yes	Yes
Torstar	1	3.5	11	Yes	No	No
Quebecor	2	2.8	9	Yes	No	No
Gesca	4	1.7	5	Yes	Yes	Yes
UniMédia	2	.9	2.7	Yes	No	No
Small chains	5	.13	.4	—	—	—
Independents	26	3.8	12	—	—	—
Total:	111	32.4				

* These numbers treat morning and evening papers owned by the same company as one newspaper.
** Businesses other than in printing, publishing and communications field.

the Winnipeg *Free Press* and the Toronto *Globe and Mail*. Thomson also acquired the Victoria *Times* and Victoria *Colonist*, the Vancouver *Sun* and Calgary *Albertan*.

The alarm mounted during the next few months. The Thomson group sold the Calgary *Albertan*, which was losing money, to the Toronto *Sun*. The Toronto *Sun* turned the *Albertan* into the Calgary *Sun*. Thomson next created a single paper, the Victoria *Times-Colonist*, from the two Victoria papers. Finally on Wednesday, August 27, 1980, the Southam chain closed the Winnipeg *Tribune*. On the same day, the Thomson group shut down the Ottawa *Journal*. Thomson then sold the Vancouver *Sun* to Southam, which already owned the other Vancouver paper, the Vancouver *Province*. Among journalists, the day came to be known as Black Wednesday. So great was the public outcry that the federal government immediately appointed a Royal Commission. The commission, headed by Professor Tom Kent, who had been a journalist and government adviser, was to investigate the newspaper industry in Canada.

The Kent Report   The Royal Commission reported in 1981. It expressed strong views on the question of ownership of the press.

The Canadian press reports a crisis in its own life.

Too much power is put in too few hands; and it is power with-out accountability. Whether the power is in practice well used or ill used or not used at all is beside the point. The point is that how it is used is subject to the indifference or to the whim of a few individuals, whether hidden or not in a faceless corporation.

Professor William Stanbury of the Economic Council of Canada made much the same point. "The record seems to indicate that both Roy Thomson and his son Ken have not interfered in the editorial policy of their newspapers. But the whole thing hinges on the good will or forbearance of one man. The temptation is great."

The publication of the Kent Commission Report did not halt the trend toward concentration of newspaper ownership. In 1982, the giant newspaper and magazine company, Maclean Hunter, bought control of the three *Sun* newspapers in Toronto, Calgary and Edmonton for $54 million.

One-newspaper Towns

One effect of the increased activity in buying and closing newspapers was to reduce the number of Canadians who have a good opportunity to read more than one newspaper. Today, only in Toronto, Winnipeg, Calgary, Edmonton, St. John's, and Halifax can English-speaking readers buy more than one local newspaper published by different owners. And in Winnipeg and Halifax, the small competing newspapers do not present a serious challenge to the large, established dailies. "In a one-newspaper town," concluded the Kent Commission, " 'freedom of the press' means nothing except the right of a proprietor to do what he will with his own."

Multi-media Ownership

Ownership is not the only matter of concern. Equally disturbing is the growing movement of newspaper owners into radio and television. There is an obvious link between all branches of the media. As the table on page 104 shows, most of the big newspaper firms have major interests in radio and television. Publishing giants are becoming broadcasting giants as well. The CTV network and CFTO-TV in Toronto were launched by the owner of the former Toronto *Telegram* newspaper. Maclean Hunter is a major shareholder in Global Communications. On a smaller scale in London, Ontario, the same family owns the London *Free Press*, radio station CFPL, and CFPL-TV.

The Canadian Radio-Television and Telecommunications Commission (CRTC), which controls broadcasting, is critical of joint newspaper and broadcasting ownership. The Kent Commission recommended that a newspaper should not be allowed to own a radio, television, or cable station in the same area as the newspaper. It also recommended that the giant Southam chain be forced to sell its radio and television interests.

The connection between newspapers and the broadcasting media is natural and easy to understand. But many of the newspapers are owned by companies that have quite different economic interests. For example, the Thomson group owns 38 daily newspapers. They also control the Hudson's Bay Company, North Sea oil and gas companies, financial and management companies, real estate companies, and many other businesses. The large Power Corporation, headed by Quebec businessman Paul Desmarais, controls Gesca. The Black family of Toronto include the Sterling newspapers as part of an enormous industrial empire. The Irving family of New Brunswick, with three dailies, greatly influences the economic life of the province with large investments in the transportation, pulp and paper, and petroleum industries. As well as many other interests in western Canada, the Sifton family also owns Armadale with two newspapers.

Mixing Oil and Newsprint

Often these companies are located in the same area as that in which the newspaper is published. Might a company's concern for its other economic interests limit the freedom of the press? Might newspapers cover news about these industries differently because their owners have millions of dollars invested in the industries?

The Canadian Daily Newspaper Publishers Association felt that there was a problem and in 1981 made its position clear.

Conflicts of interest and the appearance of conflicts of interest, must be avoided. Outside interests that could affect, or appear to affect, the newspaper's freedom to report the news impartially must be avoided.

The Kent Commission took a similar position and pointed out that ambitious editors and reporters might be tempted to avoid issues that could embarrass the paper's owners. If the owners have other business interests, the Kent Report stated, "the wells of truth are suspect." To avoid this danger, the Kent Commission recommended controls to safeguard the freedom of the editorial staff when the company that owns the newspaper also has substantial interests in other fields.

DO ADVERTISERS INFLUENCE THE PRESS?

If we paid the full cost of our newspapers or radio and television programs, this question would not arise. But we pay only about one fifth of the cost of our daily newspaper. Our taxes pay for the Canadian Broadcasting Corporation. Other radio and television programs cost us nothing. Most of the expenses involved in publishing newspapers and producing radio and television programs are met by income from advertising. All of the profits come from advertising. And, as we have seen, ownership of the mass media is profitable. Advertisers spent more than $2.1 billion on mass media in 1980: $936 million in newspapers, $600 million on television, and $388 million on radio.

Advertising and Quality

Since the media depends on money from advertising, it tries to reach the largest audience it can. Thus, in selecting and presenting the news, the media thinks not only of its importance but also of the audience it will attract. A grisly hometown murder may be "better news" in this sense than some event in Asia or Africa that could, in fact, lead to the outbreak of a war. Some offhand remark by the prime minister may

The modern newspaper depends on advertising for its income. But we also buy the newspaper because of the advertisments. Indeed, for many shoppers it might better be called the adverpaper.

receive front page coverage while an important discussion of economic policy may be buried in the back pages because it seems dull.

Dependence on income from advertising also affects the quality of writing and programs in the mass media. Since people seem to prefer "sit-coms" to Shakespeare and suspense mysteries to opera, this is what most stations provide. Such popular programs and sports events easily attract advertising sponsors.

Yet, while advertising has a bearing on the quality of programs, this does not mean it is a form of media control. It really means that we get more or less the quality of programs we want. Programs that are not listened to or watched, disappear. Newspapers that are not read, vanish.

A more serious charge often made against the press is that its dependence on income from the sale of advertising destroys or limits its freedom. Critics have suggested that newspapers or radio and television stations may hesitate to take editorial positions or publish news items that might offend major advertisers. This subject, wrote a British journalist, is "one of the most frequent questions at any meeting where newspapers are discussed." Journalists deny hotly that their papers ever give in to pressure from an advertiser, although some grant that it may have happened with others.

Advertising and Press Freedom

In 1980, a young journalist told the Kent Commission that "sometimes the ad people . . . will say to an advertiser, 'we'll get somebody to write a nice story about you too'." If a young reporter complained, he continued, the newspaper's management would just say, "you've got to accept that, that's part of it sometimes." In the same year, veteran journalist Walter Stewart, writing about the real estate section of the Toronto *Star*, said, "Reporters are instructed to write stories that are likely to persuade the reader to throw down his newspaper, rush out to his car, and drive out to look at a new subdivision — directions to which are included in each and every story."

Yet, on the whole, the Canadian media seems able to resist any pressure there might be from advertisers. In fact, advertising people complain that the media is anti-business. The president of the Canadian Institute of Advertising told the Kent Commission:

And you know, it's the view of all of the industry that we have absolutely no influence at all. And as a matter of fact, we often wish we did, because we believe that to a large extent, journalists in general — and I am not talking about newspaper journalists, I am talking about all journalists in all media, and most particularly younger ones — are extremely anti-business and hesitate not one whit in biting the hand that feeds them.

Whatever the truth, the Kent Commission reported that 72% of Canadians think that newspapers and radio and television stations do play down facts that could offend their advertisers.

HOW HAS THE GOVERNMENT RESPONDED?

During the year following Black Wednesday, the Kent Commission studied the Canadian newspaper industry. The commission concluded that "newspaper competition, of the kind that used to be, is virtually dead in Canada." There was true competition only in Toronto and in French-speaking Montreal. The commission believed that there were serious dangers to freedom of the press. The dangers were caused by big business ownership of the press, the concentration of ownership of newspapers in fewer and fewer hands, and by the expansion of newspapers into radio and television.

The reaction to the Kent Report in the boardrooms and on the editorial pages of Canadian newspapers was critical and angry. The publisher of Southam's Prince George Citizen warned: "The next step will be the government editing of all news matter. Canadians will then read and hear only what the government wants them to read and hear."

"Nice doggie — here, boy!"

The commission recommended that the government pass a law that would stop further expansion of the newspaper chains already in existence, limit the growth of new chains, and end situations where the same company owned the local newspapers and radio or television stations. It also urged the government to set up a system that would protect the independence of the editors and journalists on a newspaper owned by a company with other interests.

On May 25, 1982, the government announced that it intended to pass legislation to control media ownership. In a speech to journalism students at the University of Western Ontario, James Fleming, the minister responsible for setting up the Kent Commission, stated that Parliament would be asked to pass a law that would:

1. Prevent the growth of any new newspaper chain that would have over 20% of the national circulation. It would not force Thomson or Southam to sell any of their papers, but it would stop them from buying any new ones.

2. Prevent any non-media company from buying a newspaper unless it could guarantee that the newspaper would "be managed independently of and free from the influence of the company's other interests."

3. Direct the Canadian Radio-Television and Telecommunications Commission (CRTC), which grants television and radio licences, not to grant licences to newspapers to operate radio or television stations in the same area. (This would mean that in all probability the Armadale and Irving Companies would lose their television licences.)

Mr. Fleming also said that the government intended to create the Canadian Advisory Council on Newspapers. The Council would represent publishers, journalists, and the public, and would monitor the over-all performance of Canadian newspapers.

The proposed law was much weaker than that recommended by the Kent Commission. But it seemed to be a reasonable compromise between the uncontrolled freedom of the press to do what it wished on the one hand, and government interference that could limit freedom of the press on the other.

THE CANADIAN BROADCASTING CORPORATION: HOW WELL DOES IT PERFORM?

From time to time, some Canadians have suggested that the government should create a national newspaper, just as it did the Canadian Broadcasting Corporation (CBC). They argue that the media does not represent all shades of opinion in the country, because the owners of the media usually have the same view of things. This is generally a conservative view, to the right of the political centre. The solution would be to have the state create a newspaper that would reflect a wide range of opinion. This view has never had many supporters. As the Kent Report observed, most Canadians do not seem to care who owns the papers they read. As well, they apparently do not think the papers are one-sided. Many Canadians also fear that a government-controlled paper might be used for political propaganda.

Occasionally, people have expressed the same fears about the publicly owned CBC. But, in fact, there are more charges that the Corporation is too critical of the government than the reverse. More than twenty years ago, the government tried to cancel a CBC program because it used commentators who were critical of government policy. A strike by CBC producers defeated this attempt at government interference.

In 1980, the prime minister and members of the Liberal Party were concerned that reporters on Radio-Canada, the French-speaking section of the CBC, were too sympathetic to the separatist cause in Quebec. But, on this occasion, they ordered an independent inquiry instead of trying to interfere directly. Perhaps the government had learned from an earlier attempt at censorship. In 1975, the government had cancelled federal advertising in the separatist newspaper, Le Jour. This action had led to much criticism. The Montreal Gazette wrote, "the expression of opinion urging the independence of a province from the rest of Canada is no crime." And the Ottawa Citizen warned that "if separatism cannot be argued peacefully on the editorial page of a newspaper, then it will be argued violently in the streets."

Responsibility to Parliament

Although the CBC has a great deal of freedom in the expression of opinion, it is responsible to Parliament. The government appoints its president and directors. It does not allow the CBC to have sponsors for its news or for most current affairs programs. Although in recent years it has allowed some commercials, less than 20% of the Corporation's yearly operating costs of $700 million come from commercials. The Canadian taxpayer pays for the rest. The CBC costs each of us about eight cents a day.

The CBC says that it has a duty to honestly "hold up a mirror to the reality of the day," and tries to fulfil it. But in a recent statement, it admitted,

. . . that in the very mirroring of reality, attitudes can be influenced, perhaps in the long run even shaped. For choices have to be made as to what events will be mirrored and how they will be reflected. So it is that in the reporting of the news

the CBC emphasizes the most rigorous journalistic standards of accuracy, fairness, balance and objectivity.

The CBC's main Canadian television rivals have the same goals and ideals. An independent study published in 1978 indicated that both CBC/TV news and CTV news got high rating from their viewers. Ninety per cent of CBC viewers and 91% of CTV viewers stated that in their opinion the news was reliable.

What can we conclude about the mass media as an essential part of the political system in Canada? As the chart on page 99 indicates, more Canadians believe that television is fairer and more believable as a source of information than radio or the newspaper. However, two out of three Canadians also believe that their newspaper is doing a good or excellent job in fulfilling its responsibility to the public. At the same time, there are reasons to be concerned about the health of the press when it is a branch of big business, run for profit, and almost totally dependent on income from advertising.

Millions of Canadians get their national and international news each night from the desks of these broadcasters: (left) Knowlton Nash of the CBC, (middle) Lloyd Robertson and Harvey Kirck of CTV, and (right) Peter Trueman and Jan Tennant of Global.

STUDY GUIDE

Getting the Facts

1. Define each of the following: mass media, partisan, editorial, conflict of interest, corporation, bias, prejudice, freedom of the press.
2. Why did the government believe the Kent Commission was necessary?
3. List the main recommendations of the Kent Commission.
4. Who owns the press?

Using the Facts

1. Suggest *two* dangers of relying only on second-hand information. Is there any alternative?
2. "A free press and an unfree society cannot exist together." Do you agree?
3. Kent says that sometimes "the wells of truth are suspect." How does he believe the "wells of truth" could become polluted?
4. Why do advertisers favour newspapers over television and radio?
5. Should a national newspaper be established?
6. How does the mass media influence you? Which media influences you most...newspapers, magazines, radio, or television?
7. Eighty-nine per cent of adult Canadians read at least one newspaper a week. Does this mean that Canadians are deeply concerned about current affairs?
8. Explain the point being made in each of the cartoons in this chapter. Is there bias in any of the cartoons?
9. Draw cartoons expressing opposite points of view on the same subjects.
10. The Canadian Daily Newspaper Publishers issued this statement of principles in 1977:

    Freedom of the Press is an exercise of the common right to freedom of speech. It is the right to inform, to discuss, to advocate, to dissent. ...Truth emerges from free discussion and free reporting and both are essential to foster and preserve a democratic society.

    The newspaper has responsibilities to its readers, its shareholders, its employees and its advertisers. But the operation of a newspaper is in effect a public trust ... and its overriding responsibility is to the society which protects and provides its freedom.

The owners or publishers of some Canadian newspapers were quoted as follows:

Ken Thomson, Thomson Papers: *"I like my family's investments to grow. . .newspapers I like very much. . .look we are running a business organization. They happen to be newspapers."*

Pierre Péladeau: Le Journal de Montréal: *"The name of the game is profit. If you don't make a profit, you don't have a newspaper."*

Beland Honderich, Toronto Star: *"The shareholders of Torstar are making an investment and they will expect a return on their investment."*

To what extent are the statements of the publishers in conflict with the Statement of Principles? Do you think that the government should interfere to enforce the view that a newspaper is a "public trust?"

Research Projects

1. The Kent Commission charged that newspapers could favour business interests. For the next month, study your newspaper closely. Clip news items, editorials, and advertisements that *either* support or contradict this charge. At the end of the month, write an essay on the evidence you have collected.
2. Another charge against newspapers is that they are partisan. Can you find any evidence to support this point of view in the *political* reporting in your newspaper?
3. Collect political cartoons. What point of view is being expressed? What makes a political cartoon effective?
4. Do you think this chapter in *How Are We Governed?* is biased? What kinds of bias are there?

Chapter 7
CANADIAN FEDERALISM: HOW DOES IT WORK?

Why Does Canada Have a Federal System?
  Distribution of Power

Why Has Canada's Federal System Changed?
  Growth of Government Activities
  Health and Welfare
  Equalization
  Stabilization
  Natural Resources
  Co-operative Federalism

How Can We Change Our Federal System?
  An Unanswered Question
  The 1982 Formula

Quebec: Why Is It Different?
  The Problem
  The Solution
  Maîtres Chez Nous
  Trudeau's Answer
  Trudeau and Quebec
  Sovereignty-Association

MacPherson - TORONTO STAR

POWER TO THE PROVINCES

The view from Ottawa

MacPherson TORONTO STAR

PENNY ARCADE

The taxpayers' view

As we have seen, Canada is a federal state or federation. By this, we mean that in Canada the power to make laws is given to both a national government and to provincial governments. The British North America Act of 1867 set out this "division of powers." They are now part of the Canada Act, 1982.

WHY DOES CANADA HAVE A FEDERAL SYSTEM?

In 1867 four of the scattered British colonies in North America believed that they had to unite in order to survive and prosper. Yet none of the colonies wanted to lose completely its own identity. As a result, the colonies decided that the new united country would have a federal system of government. The national or federal government would have the power to make laws for the whole country. The colonies would become provinces in the new Dominion of Canada. The provinces would also have governments of their own to deal with matters of *local* or provincial concern.

The most difficult problem facing the Fathers of Confederation was to decide which law-making powers to give to the federal government and which to give to the provinces. Some wanted the federal government to have almost all of the powers. They wanted the government for the whole country clearly to be stronger than the provincial governments. Others believed that the provinces should have the powers needed to make them as strong as possible.

Distribution of Power

The solution finally reached by the Fathers is contained in Sections 91 to 93 of the British North America Act. In Sections 92 and 93, the Fathers listed the powers they believed the provincial governments had to have in order to protect the social and cultural identity of the people in each province. The list included, for example, control over education, language and culture, and property. The Fathers gave everything that was not included in this list to the national or central government. To show the kinds of powers they had in mind for the federal government, they gave 29 illustrations. The most important of these are listed in the table opposite.

The British North America Act makes it clear that the federal government was to have the greater power. The provincial powers and means of raising money listed in Section 92 were not nearly as important as those of the central government. In addition, the central government also had the power to *disallow*, or overturn, any provincial law that it decided was not in the interest of the country as a whole. A "disallowed" provincial law could not be enforced.

FEDERAL AND PROVINCIAL POWERS

FEDERAL

91. It shall be lawful for the Queen, by and with the Advice and Consent of the Senate and House of Commons, to make Laws for the Peace, Order, and good Government of Canada, in relation to all Matters not coming within the Classes of Subjects by this Act assigned exclusively to the Legislatures of the Provinces; . . .

[ILLUSTRATIONS]
1. The Public Debt and Property
2. The Regulation of Trade and Commerce
3. The raising of Money by any Mode or System of Taxation
5. The Postal Service
7. Militia, Military and Naval Service, and Defence
10. Navigation and Shipping
12. Sea Coast and Inland Fisheries
14. Currency and Coinage
15. Banking. . .and the Issue of Paper Money
24. Indians and Lands reserved for Indians
25. Naturalization and Aliens
26. Marriage and Divorce
27. The Criminal Law

PROVINCIAL

92. . . .
1. The Amendment. . .of the Constitution. . .except as regards the Office of Lieutenant-Governor
2. Direct Taxation within the Province. . .
5. The Management and Sale of the Public Lands. . .
8. Municipal Institutions in the Province
9. Shop, Saloon, Tavern, Auctioneer, and other licences
10. Local Works and Undertaking other than such as are of the following Classes:
   a) Transportation facilities linking two provinces
   b) Transportation facilities linking Canada and other countries
   c) Facilities which the Parliament of Canada declares to be for the welfare of Canada or more than the single province.
12. The Solemnization of Marriage. . .
13. Property and Civil rights. . .
14. The Administration of Justice. . .
16. Generally all Matters of a merely local or private Nature. . .

93. In and for each Province the legislature may exclusively make laws in relation to Education. . . .

The federal government also had the right to appoint, and to fire, the Lieutenant Governors, who were the formal heads of each provincial government. Among the duties of the Lieutenant Governors was that of reporting to Ottawa on the activities of the provincial governments. Under Section 92:10 of the British North America Act, the federal government could also take over provincial roads, canals, or railways if it were in the national interest to do so. The provinces had control over education. But the central government had the power to protect the educational rights of religious minorities—the Protestants in Quebec and the Roman Catholics elsewhere.

In these ways, the Fathers of Confederation created a *highly centralized* federal system. That is, they created a system in which the central government in Ottawa had by far the most important powers.

WHY HAS CANADA'S FEDERAL SYSTEM CHANGED?

During the past century, however, Canada's highly centralized federal system has changed a great deal. These changes reflect equally great changes in the country itself. Canada today is not much like the Canada of Confederation. The parent-child relationship between the central government and the provinces no longer exists. Often the provincial children seem powerful enough to do battle on equal terms with the federal parent.

Growth of Government Activities

The most important single reason is that all governments today play a much larger role in the world than they did a century ago. As we have seen, it is very difficult to think of any of our everyday activities that does not involve government in some way. One of the best examples of this larger role is the greatly increased amount of the country's total wealth that the national, provincial, and local governments spend. The total wealth of our country is the value of all the goods and services we produce in Canada. This is known as the *Gross National Product* or *GNP*. Through the taxes we pay, the government is able to use this wealth.

There are no accurate figures for 1867. An educated guess would be that governments then spent much less than 5% of the country's wealth or GNP. In 1926, when Canada began to keep accurate records, governments spent 16%. By 1962, government spending had risen to 30%. Today, governments in Canada spend about 45% of GNP. Of that total amount, the provincial and local governments spend about 65%. The federal government spends the rest.

What explains the enormous growth in government activity and spending since Confederation? In 1867 Canada was a small country. Most people lived on the family farm or in small towns. There were few cities of any size. Life centred on the family, which was usually large. The family, often helped by neighbours, was expected to look after its own sick and elderly, poor and unemployed. There were a few railways, but the main links between towns and villages were dirt roads,

GROWTH IN GOVERNMENT EXPENDITURES*
AS PERCENTAGE OF GROSS NATIONAL PRODUCT

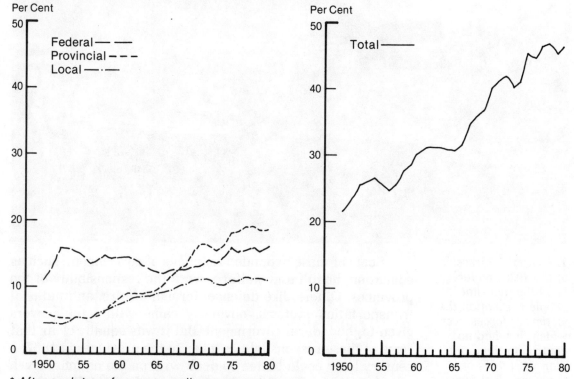

* *After cash transfers among all governments.*
Source: Statistics Canada, National Income and Expenditure Accounts.

often little more than tracks. Most students did not have a chance to go to high school. Few even dreamed of attending a university. There was a small army in the country, but Britain at that time still controlled Canada's foreign policy. Few Canadians thought that it was the business of government to make rich and poor citizens or rich and poor parts of the country more equal.

In the twentieth century, particularly since the Great Depression of the 1930s, these conditions have all changed greatly. Canada is no longer a nation made up mainly of farmers. It is an industrial country marked by great cities in which huge factories employ thousands of workers. The family is no longer able to look after its members. Governments have had to take on the main responsibility for helping the less fortunate members of society. As life became more complex, citizens needed much more education in order to live effectively. Canada took part in two world wars, and as a completely independent nation had to take a much greater part in world affairs. To pay for these and many other new activities, the government had to increase taxes on our incomes, on company profits, and on almost everything we buy.

The Great Depression of the 1930s underlined the fact that people were often the victims of forces over which they had no control. In the Canadian west, tens of thousands fled farms that drought had turned into dust bowls. In the cities, tens of thousands lost their jobs and moved restlessly around the country looking for employment.

Some of these expanded functions of government, such as education, health and welfare, were the responsibility of the provinces. Others, like defence, foreign affairs, and national transportation systems, obviously came within the powers given to the federal government. But it was equally clear that some of those responsibilities given to the provinces in 1867, a century later could better be dealt with on the national level.

A century after Confederation, Canadians realized that a federal system designed for an agricultural country in 1867 was no longer adequate for a society that had changed as much as Canada has. But it has proved much more difficult to change our federal system than to point out its weaknesses. An examination of just a few of the most important issues will show how difficult it has been to make the Canadian federal system work better in a changing country and a changing world.

Health and Welfare

As we pointed out, a century ago most Canadians believed that it was the duty of one's family and neighbours to look after those who were poor or unemployed, sick or old. People did not expect the government to help and the government made few offers to do so. This view changed as a result of a number of developments during this century. The growth of industry and the movement of people to the cities created problems and needs that were too great for families or neighbours to deal with. The Great Depression of the 1930s underlined the need for government action as Canada suffered nation-wide unemployment and distress. Increasingly, Canadians came to believe that the individual or the family should not have to pay the entire cost of health and welfare. Society as a whole should share the costs. Canadians also came to believe that everyone in the country should have roughly the same amount of protection and benefits. However, there was a problem in this regard. The British North America Act gave the provinces control over matters of social welfare. In 1867, when the four British colonies joined Confederation, few thought that there would be social problems and needs that would affect everyone in the country.

One of the earliest attempts to get around the problem occurred in 1927. In that year the provinces agreed that the federal government should set up a national system of old-age pensions. In 1940 the federal government also took on responsibility for the unemployed. The Depression had made it clear that unemployment was a national problem, not just a provincial one. After the Second World War, both the federal and provincial governments agreed that there was need for a public medical and hospital insurance program. Although health care was a provincial responsibility, the federal government agreed to pay half the cost of the provincial health care programs. But each province had to agree that its program would meet stated national standards.

Medicare and hospital insurance became known as "shared cost programs." The provinces ran the programs, but the federal government and the provinces each paid a share of the cost. After 1945 the number of such programs increased. Ottawa agreed to share the cost of helping the blind, disabled, and elderly. It also helped support the growing number of universities in all the provinces. Between 1977 and 1982 alone, Ottawa "transferred" more than $50 billion to the provinces in support of such programs.

Some provincial leaders have argued that the federal government should leave control of these matters entirely to the provinces. Ottawa should not pay any part of the cost of such programs. Instead the federal government would tax the people less and let the provinces have the extra taxes. The federal government does not agree. It believes that such a policy would make it impossible for the national government to carry out two very important responsibilities: *equalization* and *stabilization*. These words describe policies of basic importance in understanding Canadian federalism.

Equalization

In simple terms, *equalization* is a policy designed to make sure that people in every Canadian province have roughly the same standard of living, social services, and educational opportunities. The policy is meant to make sure that no Canadian suffers unusual hardships simply because of where he or she lives in the country.

The different provinces or regions in Canada have always been unequal in wealth. As the bar graph shows, there are great differences today in the per capita income in each of the ten provinces. If each province had to provide social welfare programs on its own, the standard of living, educational opportunities, and social services would be very unequal across the country.

LEVELS OF PROVINCIAL INCOME PER CAPITA, 1980

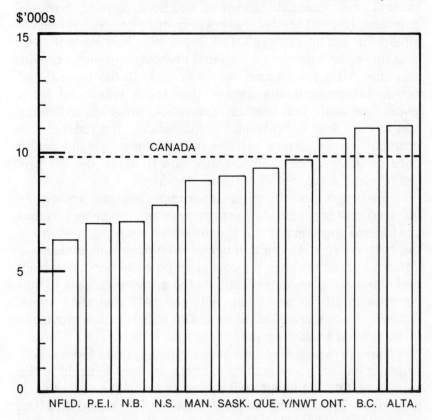

$'000s

To prevent such inequality, the federal government and the provinces agreed in the 1950s to a policy of equalization. Each year, Ottawa makes a payment to the poorer provinces to help them provide essential services for their people. Such payments ensure more or less equal services for all Canadians without those in the poorer provinces having to pay much higher taxes than those in the richer provinces. In this sense, Ottawa takes money from the richer provinces and gives it to the poorer.

Equalization payments have been called "the glue" that holds Canada together. They amounted to $3.4 billion in

1980-81. Without this money, the Atlantic provinces, Manitoba, and Quebec would have had great difficulty in meeting the needs of their residents. The equalization policy is so important to the well-being of many Canadians that the Constitution Act of 1982 contains a clause that makes it necessary for the federal government to continue the policy.

At the same time as it makes equalization payments, the federal government tries to find ways to lessen the need for the equalization policy. For example, it tries to stimulate greater economic development in the poorer regions of the country. It gives grants to companies to set up or expand industries in poorer regions. As well, it supports the provinces in a wide range of economic activities. Between 1977 and 1982, such aid to the provinces amounted to $2.1 billion.

FEDERAL TRANSFER PAYMENTS TO THE PROVINCES PER CAPITA, 1980-81

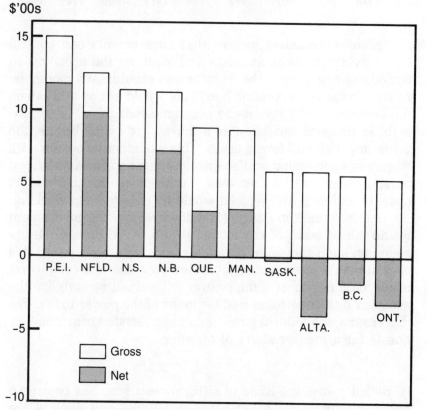

Source: Economic Council of Canada, Financing Confederation, 1982.

Every province receives payments from Ottawa for shared cost and a variety of other programs. The total federal payments to the provinces are called gross payments. But the residents of each province also pay taxes to the federal government. If we subtract the amount paid in taxes by residents in each province from the gross payments paid to the province, we get a figure for net transfer payments. These net payments show that some of the wealth of the country is transferred from the richer to the poorer provinces.

Stabilization is a policy by which the federal government, like governments elsewhere in the world, tries to keep the country's economy running smoothly. Like stabilizers on ships or aircraft, the stabilization policy is designed to keep our

Stabilization

economic system as level as possible in the face of economic waves and winds. Left to itself, a modern economic system is not stable or level. It does not move along evenly or steadily. Rather, as the chart shows, it fluctuates or swings in an up-and-down motion through good times to bad times when many are unemployed.

GROSS NATIONAL PRODUCT

Source: Statistics Canada

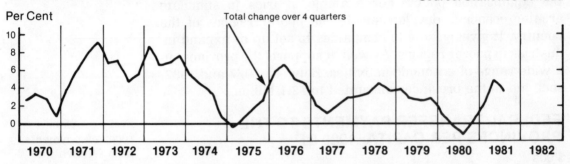

The shifts in the value of our Gross National Product is one sign of the lack of stability in the economy. Governments would prefer to see a much straighter line.

Many economists believe that governments can control these swings so as to stabilize and level out the economy. In periods of prosperity, the government should save money by raising taxes and spending less. This would act as a brake on the economy and prevent the economic swing from going too high. In times of recession as a downward swing begins, the government should lower taxes. This would leave people with more money to spend and so create a demand for appliances, cars, or clothes. In this way, factories could continue to operate and men and women would be able to keep working.

At the same time during the down swing, the government would spend some of the money it had saved during the upswing on such things as roads, airports, and housing. In this way, it would create more jobs. However, the federal government could not control the swings to level out or stabilize the economy if the provinces had too much of the power to tax. For this reason, the federal government has resisted provincial requests for a greater share of taxation.

Natural Resources

In recent years, the issue of natural resources has become a growing source of conflict between Ottawa and some of the provinces. The provinces own the natural resources on their land and under it. Some provinces, particularly Alberta, but also British Columbia and Saskatchewan, have earned huge amounts of money from the development of their oil and gas resources. These provinces believe that most of this money should remain in the province. Ottawa, on the other hand,

In one form or another, the question of natural resources has been before the courts for many years. The latest issue [1982] to go before the Supreme Court is the owner- ship of resources off the shores of New- foundland.

believes that all Canadians should benefit. As a result, the federal government has used its powers to tax the oil com- panies and to control the selling price of oil and gas outside the province to take part of this provincial income. Ottawa has also used its power to control prices to keep the price of oil and gas in Canada lower than it is in the world market. If it had not done so and Alberta had received the world price for its oil in 1980, that province would have been $13 billion richer. The rest of Canada would have been $13 billion poorer. Put another way, each Albertan could have been about $6500 richer and every other Canadian about $600 poorer.

With such great sums of money at stake, it is not surpris- ing that the issue of the development and taxation of natural resources brings Ottawa and the oil-rich provinces into head- on collisions. Those provinces without oil usually support Ot- tawa's position that part of the profits from oil resources should benefit the nation as a whole. Provinces that hope to find oil off their shores, like Newfoundland and Nova Scotia, are sympathetic to the position of the oil provinces. At the same time, however, the oil provinces do not deny that some of the profits should benefit all Canadians. The question is, how much?

Federal and provincial politicians have dealt with the above and many other important issues without really changing the division of powers set out in the British North America Act.

Co-operative Federalism

WHERE DO YOU STAND?

ASK YOURSELF THESE QUESTIONS:

1. Should all Canadians have the same level of such social services as medical and hospital care? Old-age pensions? Unemployment insurance?
2. Should all Canadians earning the same amount of money pay the same amount of taxes?
3. Should income from such natural resources as oil, gas and hydroelectricity benefit the entire country?
4. Should there be roughly the same curriculum in schools across Canada?
5. Should there be a national university system?
6. Should the national government alone control foreign policy?
7. Should Canadians be able to work and own property in any province?
8. Should the federal government have complete control over radio and television broadcasting?
9. Should the federal government alone control immigration policy?
10. Should the federal government alone appoint the judges on the Supreme Court of Canada which must make decisions about the powers of the federal and provincial governments?

NO   YES

|ı|ı|ı|ı|ı|ı|ı|ı|ı|ı|ı|ı|ı|ı|ı|ı|ı|ı|ı|ı|ı|ı|ı|
▲

Decentralized   Centralized

The number of Yes and No answers will indicate where you stand on the question of the balance of power in the Canadian federal system.

Through discussion and negotiation, they have taken a nineteenth-century system and tried to make it fit the needs of the twentieth century. In the process, the prime ministers meet frequently during the year. And there are hundreds of meetings between federal and provincial cabinet ministers and civil servants. This system of continuous discussion and negotiation has been called "co-operative federalism." But so frequent are the clashes and loud the threats and accusations, that many question the accuracy of the adjective co-operative.

Some Canadians believe that it is time to draw up a new division of powers. At a number of conferences, federal and provincial leaders have tried to do just that. They have never been able to reach agreement. Ottawa does not want to give up too much of its power to tax and spend. The poorer provinces do not want the federal government so weakened that it cannot help them. Even the wealthier provinces have not been able to agree on which powers should be provincial and which national. In all the debates and discussions, Quebec has been determined to get so much power for the provinces that there seemed little left for the national government to do. The Canadian people, like their leaders, seemed confused and uncertain and unable to reach agreement.

HOW CAN WE CHANGE OUR FEDERAL SYSTEM?

Canadians have not only not been able to agree on *what* changes to make in the division of powers between federal and provincial governments. They have also had great difficulty in agreeing on *how* to make any such changes. The British North America Act stated that the government of the United Kingdom could change the act if the Canadian Parliament asked it to do so. The Canadian Parliament had the right to make such a request on its own. But it has been accepted practice not to ask for any amendment to the act that affected relations between the provinces and the federal government without consultation and agreement with the provinces.

It was not clear, however, exactly what was involved in such consultation and agreement. For example, did all the provinces have to agree or only a majority of them? Did tiny Prince Edward Island have the same rights as Quebec? Could Ottawa act alone if, after consultation, there was no agreement? For many years, these and many other questions remained unanswered. Thus, there was no agreement on a formula for changing or amending the constitution.

An Unanswered Question

The 1982 Formula

In 1982, as part of its new constitution "package," the Trudeau government finally won the agreement of all provinces except Quebec to an amending formula. The Constitution Act, 1982, states that amendments to the constitution can be made after approval by the Canadian Parliament and by the legislatures of two thirds of the provinces provided they have fifty per cent of the population. However, if an amendment reduces the power of a province, the provincial government can declare that the amendment will not apply to that province. If an amendment transfers educational or cultural matters from some of the provinces, the Canadian government will pay to those provinces which do not agree to the transfer, enough money to repay them for providing the services themselves. Any amendment affecting the monarchy or the Supreme Court requires the agreement of all provinces and the federal government.

Although nine provincial governments accepted the amending formula, few thought that it was perfect. The Quebec government refused to accept it at all. The main reason for this refusal was that the formula did not give Quebec the right to veto or throw out an amendment. Quebec felt that without such a veto it could not protect its language and culture. As a result, the Constitution Act provided that the prime ministers should meet within fifteen years to review the amending formula.

After the new constitution came into effect, the Quebec government declared that any formula for amending the constitution that does not give Quebec a veto over any change that might effect the province will never be acceptable to it.

QUEBEC: WHY IS IT DIFFERENT?

In 1976, the Quebec voters surprised most Canadians by electing the Parti Québecois. Led by René Lévesque, the *péquistes* as they are known, called for the political independence of Quebec. Quebec would no longer be a part of Canada and would be free to make whatever laws it wished on any matter. However, Lévesque promised that an independent Quebec would form an economic association or union with the rest of Canada. This meant that in such matters as trade, for example, the two countries, Quebec and Canada, would act as one. The reasons for this promise was the recognition that Quebec independence would be very costly. Lévesque also promised that before the province separated he would ask Quebec voters to approve the policy of independence combined with association in a referendum. What explains the success of the Parti Québecois?

November 15, 1976. Jubilant Parti Québecois supporters learn that their party has swept to victory. But all public opinion polls indicated that many of those who had voted for the Parti Québecois did not support independence.

The Problem

More than 80% of Quebec's population is French-speaking. More than 60% speak only French. Ever since the British conquest in 1760, the people of Quebec, the Québecois, have had one main concern: *la survivance* — survival. In 1867 the Québecois accepted Confederation. They did so without enthusiasm and only after they felt assured that the new provincial government would have enough powers to ensure their survival as a people.

Quebec remained uneasy in the Canadian federal system. Outside the province, English was the language of the country. Increasingly, Ottawa, the nation's capital, became an English-speaking capital. In Ontario and the Prairie provinces, French-language schools were under attack. Within Quebec itself, the minority of English-speaking inhabitants controlled industry, trade, and finance. French Canadians had to learn English in order to get ahead in business. Without a knowledge of the language of business, French Canadians remained "hewers of wood and drawers of water" in their own province. Finally, whenever French and English differed on such major national issues as the execution in 1885 of the Metis leader Louis Riel, the protection of French schools, or conscription in the two world wars the French-Canadian minority always lost.

The Solution

These experiences caused French Canadians to look inward upon themselves and their own Quebec. For decades, their political leaders defended the walls of "fortress Quebec" against real or imagined attacks by the federal government.

But by the 1950s many Quebecers were convinced that

only major changes in their government and society could ensure their survival. In the 1960 election, the reform forces triumphed and Jean Lesage formed a Liberal government dedicated to widespread change. A prominent member of that government was René Lévesque.

For the next fifteen years a number of Quebec governments carried out many important reforms within the province. These included new labour laws, social legislation, and basic changes in the educational system from kindergarten to university. The government also began to play a much more active part in the provincial economy.

History has often divided French and English in Canada, rather than united them. Too often, as well, the teaching of Canadian history and politics in both cultures has not aided mutual understanding.

Maîtres Chez Nous

There was another element in the reform movement that affected not only Quebec but all of Canada. The slogan of the movement was *maîtres chez nous*, masters in our own house. This slogan underlined the Québecois' conviction that their province was not like the others. Quebec was a distinct and separate society. It had its own people, its own history, its own culture, its own resources, and its own government.

From 1960 to the present, the Quebec government and people have been working out in practice the ideas of *maîtres chez nous*. Increasingly, the government became involved in the economy to advance the interests of the Québecois. It demanded more tax revenue from the federal government in Ottawa. Quebec also demanded and won the right to "*opt out*" of most federal-provincial programs. This meant that Quebec would receive from the federal government the money for such programs as old-age pensions, medical and hospital care, and family allowances. But it would run the programs on its own.

Throughout this period most English-speaking Canadians were puzzled. Just what kind of federal system did Quebec want? One difficulty was that the Québecois themselves answered the question differently. There was no single answer. Some Québecois wanted a federal system in which Quebec, and the other provinces if they wished, had very much more power and revenue than at present. The federal government would be reduced to a mere shadow of its former position. The provinces would even control some areas of foreign policy. Some Québecois pushed further. They maintained that Canada was two nations, one French, one English. Therefore, there should be a new federal system with two equal *associated states*, one French, one English. At the extreme were those Québecois who believed that the only satisfactory long-range solution was complete independence for Quebec.

Among those who were convinced that political independence was the only permanent solution was René Lévesque. One year after the centennial of Canadian Confederation, in 1968, Lévesque formed the Parti Québecois, which stood for independence from Canada, but, if possible, with some kind of economic association.

In 1968 Pierre Trudeau became prime minister of Canada. He had a totally different answer than René Lévesque. Trudeau believed that Quebec had to come closer to the rest of Canada, not leave the country. He argued that Quebec should not be allowed to "opt out" of federal-provincial programs, or sooner or later Quebec for many practical purposes would be a separate state. More important, he maintained that the Québecois must be made to feel at home and have equal opportunities everywhere in Canada. If Canada were truly bilingual and bicultural, the separatist movement would lose most of its strength.

The key to Prime Minister Trudeau's policy was language. A Royal Commission on Bilingualism and Biculturalism had reported in the late 1960s that although the British North America Act had stated that French and English were to be used in the Canadian Parliament and courts, English was really the language of work in the national capital. For example, only 14% of senior civil servants were French-speaking, although 28% of the population was Francophone. Elsewhere in Canada, except Quebec and New Brunswick (which was 35% French-speaking) the situation was much worse. Even in

Trudeau's Answer

THE OCTOBER CRISIS, 1970

While René Lévesque pressed for the separation of Quebec by democratic and peaceful means, there were others who adopted the tactics of violence and revolution. The most important was the Front de libération du Québec, or the FLQ. The FLQ began its war of terror to win an independent and socialistic Quebec in 1963. By 1970, it had committed dozens of robberies to get money, dynamite, and arms. Five people had been killed and many others wounded as the FLQ placed bombs in mailboxes, homes, and buildings. All separatists were encouraged by the French president General de Gaulle, who shouted "Vivre le Québec libre" when he visited Montreal in 1967.

On the morning of October 5, 1970, one cell of the FLQ created the famous October Crisis when it kidnapped James Cross, a British diplomat in Montreal. The kidnappers issued a statement. They demanded the release of imprisoned FLQ members, $500 000 in gold, the publication of their manifesto calling for the independence of a radical, socialist Quebec, and their safe passage to Cuba. As the police searched frantically for Cross, the federal and Quebec governments agreed only to read the manifesto on television.

Most Canadians supported the hard line adopted by the two governments. But there were many radical separatists who attempted to stir up support for the kidnappers. Tension grew on October 10 when another FLQ cell kidnapped Pierre Laporte, a Quebec cabinet minister. By October 14, the supporters of the FLQ were organizing massive strikes and demonstrations. Believing that it could not keep public order, and unable to find the kidnappers, the Quebec government asked the federal government to send in the army to reinforce the Quebec police and help maintain law and order. Montrealers woke up on October 15 to find they lived in an occupied city.

A day later, October 16, the federal government declared that Quebec faced a possible uprising (an "apprehended insurrection") and approved the use of the War Measures Act. This act suspended legal rights (see pages 172-3) and gave the police extraordinary powers to arrest and jail anyone suspected of being a member of, or sympathizing with, the FLQ.

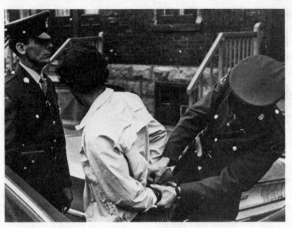

Within hours, hundreds of separatists, suspected sympathizers, and, as it turned out, completely innocent people were roused from their beds, picked up in the streets, and arrested. Most Canadians, inside Quebec and out, believed that the FLQ had to be crushed. But there were many who felt that the use of the War Measures Act was a tragic attack on the legal rights or civil liberties that Canadians believe they should have except in the case of a war.

(Below) The presence of the army and the use of the War Measures Act brought a troubled quiet to Quebec. But the Laporte kidnappers replied by strangling their captive. The police search continued, and on December 3, James Cross was found. In return for his life, the government escorted his kidnappers to a Montreal airport where a waiting airplane took them to Cuba. After a few years, they tired of Castro's Cuba, which they had so admired, and moved to France. In the end, one by one, they returned to Canada, where they were tried, found guilty, and sent to prison.

(Right) Finally, on December 28, Paul Rose and the other kidnappers of Pierre Laporte were captured. Rose, shown here arriving at court, was found guilty of the murder of Laporte and sentenced to life imprisonment. Other members of the cell were also found guilty and imprisoned.

At the time, the October Crisis seemed to hurt the reputation of the Parti Québecois, for some Canadians did not distinguish between the democratic means used by René Lévesque and the tactics of murder and kidnapping adopted by the FLQ. But as time passed, many people remembered only the trampling of civil liberties and forgot the barbarous acts that had seemed to make the use of the War Measures Act necessary.

Ontario and Manitoba, with a significant Francophone minority, French Canadians did not always find it easy to get an education in French. In other provinces it was almost impossible.

In 1969 the Trudeau government passed the official Languages Act. The act stated:

The English and French languages are the official languages of Canada for all purposes of the Parliament and the Government of Canada and possess and enjoy equality of status and equal rights and privileges as to their use in all the institutions of the Parliament and Government of Canada.

The law did not mean that all civil servants had to be bilingual. It did, however, increase opportunities for Francophones and greatly improved the chances of those who were bilingual. The government encouraged civil servants to become bilingual and spent millions of dollars on French- and English-language education. Federal offices used both languages wherever there were English- or French-speaking minorities.

"It's a great success – eight percent of them learn to swim."

There was intense opposition to the policy of bilingualism in many parts of Canada. Moreover, there were many who doubted that the program was a success in Ottawa itself. In 1978, the official responsible for supervising the program declared that he would only give the government a C plus. Only 10% of the civil servants who graduated from language school, he said, could in fact work in the French language.

Prime Minister Trudeau wanted to go farther than the Official Languages Act. His goal was to have the provinces, which controlled education, provide schooling in French. If this were the case, French Canadians would be able to feel at home in any part of Canada. It would also remove what Trudeau believed was a real injustice and a sign of inequality between French- and English-speaking Canadians. For years he battled with most of the English-speaking provinces. These provinces either disagreed with the proposal in principle or felt that the costs of putting it into effect were too great.

Trudeau and Quebec

Prime Minister Trudeau also had to battle with Quebec. On the question of language that province was heading in a different direction. The supporters of *maîtres chez nous* believed that the language of the province had to be that of the vast majority of its people: French. This seemed not only to be just; it was also the only way French-speaking Quebecers would have equal opportunity in the world of industry, business, and finance in Quebec. Many in Quebec were also concerned that the majority of immigrants, and even some French Canadians, sent their children to English-language schools. Since the birthrate among French Canadians in Quebec was falling, some people predicted that in time Montreal would cease to be a French-speaking city, if parents could choose either English- or French-language schools for their children.

Since the 1960s, Quebec governments had passed laws increasing the use of the French language in government, business, and education. A year after his election in 1976, Premier Lévesque went further and passed Bill 101. This bill:

(1) made French the only official language of Quebec, including the legislature, all government bodies and the courts. (This clause, in effect, challenged the BNA Act, which guaranteed equality of both French and English in the legislature and courts of Quebec.)

(2) limited English-language education to those children of Quebec parents whose mother tongue was English. (This clause denied the right of children of "immigrants" from outside Canada as well as those from other parts of Canada to choose the language of education. Business leaders protested that other Canadians would refuse to work in Quebec. As a result, the government agreed that temporary residents could send their children to English schools for three years.)

(3) ordered all stores and businesses to have all their signs and advertisements in French only.

(4) provided that all companies with more than 50 employees make French the language of work.

Bill 101 angered English-speaking Quebecers. They immediately appealed to the courts on the grounds that Bill 101 went against the terms of the BNA Act. In 1981 the Supreme Court of Canada ruled that the section of Bill 101 that made French the only official language in the legislature and the courts was not legal since the BNA Act guaranteed the equality of both languages in the legislature and courts of Quebec.

Quebec's language legislation also angered Prime Minister Trudeau. He became even more determined to include a guarantee for minority language education rights in the *Charter of Rights and Freedoms* in Canada's new constitution.

Although the Parti Québecois passed a number of important measures, it did not lose sight of its main objective: the political independence of Quebec and some form of economic union with Canada. Lévesque defined the goal as "sovereignty-association." As it prepared for the referendum, or vote, on the question, the Lévesque government worked hard to calm those who were anxious and worried about what the future held under "sovereignty-association." It promised not to negotiate independence unless the rest of Canada had first accepted an economic association. The government also played down the whole idea of independence. The official Parti Québecois statement was called "Quebec-Canada: A New Deal." Its subtitle spoke of "a new partnership between equals." Finally, in the referendum, the government asked only for the right to negotiate an agreement with Ottawa. The people would have a chance to approve the agreement in another referendum. Every effort was made to lessen any feeling of alarm.

Sovereignty-Association

The opponents of sovereignty-association argued that the economic costs of independence for Quebec would be disastrously high. Besides, English Canada would never agree to an economic association. Some Quebecers pointed out that a person could be a good Québecois, proud of the unique society and at the same time be a good Canadian. Slogans on buttons — "Choose Quebec and Canada" and *Mon Non est Québecois* — made the point. Prime Minister Trudeau entered the contest to proclaim his Canadianism and to promise important changes in the federal system.

On May 20, 1980, 59.5% of those who voted said No to Premier Lévesque's proposal. English-speaking Quebecers voted overwhelmingly no. But Francophones also voted No by a small majority in almost every section of the province, including Quebec City and Montreal. For the moment Lévesque admitted defeat. A year later his government easily won another provincial election on issues other than independence.

Montreal Gazette,
April 30, 1980

REFERENDUM GYMNASTICS

Showing a few of the twists and turns Mr. Lévesque uses to avoid using that awful word "Independence"

Although the Parti Québecois remained committed to independence for Quebec, the issue might not have surfaced again for a number of years. However, the struggle over the new constitution gave it renewed life and importance in the province. For years Quebec had fought against *patriation* of the BNA Act; that is, the removal of the British Parliament from playing any part in changing Canada's constitution. Quebec had also opposed a bill of rights for Canada. Before it would agree to either, Quebec insisted that there had to be agreement on a new division of powers to give the provinces more power. There also had to be a method of amending the constitution that would, in effect, give Quebec a veto.

In 1981, Ottawa and the other provinces finally reached an agreement on patriation and a Charter of Rights and Free-

SOVEREIGNTY-ASSOCIATION

QUE.

doms. This agreement denied both of Quebec's demands. The government of Quebec refused to accept the agreement and immediately introduced legislation to try to make certain that the new constitution would have no effect in Quebec. To Lévesque and his supporters, the struggle over the constitution proved that their position had been right all along: independence was the only way to guarantee the survival of Quebec as a distinctive society. As Canadians elsewhere celebrated the proclamation of the new constitution on April 17, 1982, René Lévesque and the *péquistes* marched in solemn protest through the streets of Montreal.

May 20, 1980:
She didn't get up.

The future of the Canadian federal system has yet to be determined. Quebec, a province unlike the others, may never separate, but it will continue to demand increased powers. So too, from time to time, will other provincial governments. On the other hand, many Canadians will continue to argue that the central government is already too weak, and that any further weakening of power at the centre will endanger Canada's unity and strength.

STUDY GUIDE

Getting the Facts

1. Define each of the following: division of powers, federal, disallowance, centralization, the Great Depression, medicare, equalization, stabilization, world price, co-operative federalism, veto, péquistes, referendum, *la survivance, maîtres chez nous,* "opt out," bilingual, bicultural, quiet revolution, Québecois, two nations theory, associated states, separatist, FLQ crisis, Official Languages Act, Francophone, Anglophone, Bill 101, sovereignty-association, patriation.
2. In what ways was Canadian federalism in 1867 similar to a parent/child relationship?
3. Why has Canadian federalism changed?
4. Why did "shared cost programs" become necessary?
5. Why has the equalization policy been called "the glue" that holds Canada together?
6. What is the purpose of the stabilization policy? How does it work?
7. What is the formula for amending the Canadian constitution?
8. Why have many French Canadians become dissatisfied with their place in the Canadian federal system?
9. Why do many French Canadians think that the Canada Act, 1982, is unacceptable?

Using the Facts

1. Explain the reasons for your answers to the ten questions on "Where Do You Stand," page 128.
2. Do you believe that the Quebec government was justified in passing Bill 101?
3. Do you think that Quebec should have the same position as any other province in the Canadian federal system? Explain your answer.

Research Projects

1. Some provinces believe that there should be a new distribution of powers between the federal and provincial governments. Find out what proposals your provincial government has made during the past decade. (Your provincial ministry of intergovernmental affairs should be able to provide the information.) Do you support the position your provincial government has taken on such matters as: the distribution of power, taxation, the Senate, appointments to the Supreme Court?
2. It is difficult to understand the view that many French Canadians have of Canadian federalism without understanding the significance of a number of crises in the relations between Quebec and the rest of the country. Using a general history of

Canada, discover the importance of the following events in shaping the relations between Quebec and English-speaking Canada.

a) The execution of Louis Riel, 1885
b) The Manitoba Schools Question, 1890-97
c) The Boer War, 1899-1902
d) The Conscription Crisis, 1917
e) The Quebec Election, 1939
f) The Conscription Plebiscite, 1942

Chapter 8
PROVINCIAL AND LOCAL GOVERNMENTS: WHAT ROLE DO THEY PLAY?

Are Provincial Governments Different?
Political System
Political Parties
Parliamentary Government
Provincial Differences

What Do the Provincial Governments Do?
Provincial Income and Expenditure
Local Government

Why Have Local Government?
Urban Growth
New Responsibilities
Local Responsibilities

How Are Local Governments Organized?
Ontario
British Columbia
Municipal Finance

Local Government: The Cradle of Democracy?

(Opposite) To school, at school, and after school, we live in the shade of provincial and local governments.

In earlier chapters we have dealt mainly with government at the national level, the government common to all Canadians. Yet, as we have seen, the power to pass the laws that affect our lives is divided between a national government and the ten provincial governments. In many ways, the powers that the provincial governments possess affect us more on a day-to-day basis than those given to the national government. In the long run, whether we are at peace or war, or whether our standard of living is affected by poor national economic policies is of the greatest importance. But every day we use highways or streetcars, go to school or visit a sick relative in the hospital, put out the garbage and turn on the lights. And the responsibility for our highways and public transit systems, schools and hospitals, and all our public utilities belong to the provincial and local governments. These responsibilities may be less exciting than foreign affairs or defence, international trade, or constitutional reform, but they are no less important.

ARE PROVINCIAL GOVERNMENTS DIFFERENT?

The system of government in the Canadian provinces works in much the same way as on the national level. Almost everything written in the chapters on the political system, democracy, parliamentary government, and political parties is much the same for the provinces.

Political System

Of course, the provincial political systems are less difficult to understand than the national system because the environment is much less complicated. Most provinces are part of one geographic region. The people who settled there share a common history. In many provinces, there is not the great mixture of people that we find in the country as a whole; in others almost all peoples and creeds can be found. The role of government, the decision-makers as we called them, remains the same. The provincial governments, too, must meet the needs of the people and respond to their demands in ways that find popular acceptance.

Political Parties

The role of the mass media, the pressure groups, and the political parties are the same. Provincial political parties usually have the same names as those on the federal level — Liberal, Progressive Conservative, New Democratic Party. Many people belong to the same party on both the national and provincial level. But the provincial and national parties have separate leaders and, on the whole, separate organizations. Many people vote for one party in a national election and another party on the provincial level. While the NDP has never won a national election, it has won elections and become the government in British Columbia, Saskatchewan, and Manitoba. It has also come close in Ontario. The Social Credit party, which has disappeared from the national arena, governed Alberta from 1935 to 1971. It is still a force in British Columbia, where it formed the government from 1952 to 1972, and has been in power again since 1975. In Quebec, a na-

THE ONTARIO PARLIAMENTARY SYSTEM

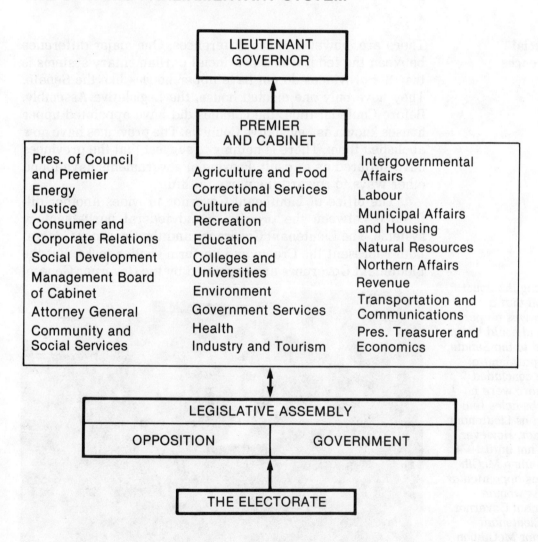

LIEUTENANT GOVERNOR

PREMIER AND CABINET

Pres. of Council and Premier
Energy
Justice
Consumer and Corporate Relations
Social Development
Management Board of Cabinet
Attorney General
Community and Social Services

Agriculture and Food
Correctional Services
Culture and Recreation
Education
Colleges and Universities
Environment
Government Services
Health
Industry and Tourism

Intergovernmental Affairs
Labour
Municipal Affairs and Housing
Natural Resources
Northern Affairs
Revenue
Transportation and Communications
Pres. Treasurer and Economics

LEGISLATIVE ASSEMBLY

OPPOSITION | GOVERNMENT

THE ELECTORATE

tionalist party called the Union Nationale was in power for most of the time between 1935 and 1960, and the even more nationalist Parti Québecois has been in power since 1976.

Parliamentary Government

Finally, the provinces also enjoy parliamentary government. The same responsibility of the executive (or Cabinet) to the legislature exists. No government can remain in office without the support of a majority of the elected members. The premier forms the Cabinet in the same way and, if a strong leader, dominates the Cabinet and the party. All bills must be approved by the legislature to become laws.

Provincial Differences

There are, however, some differences. One major difference between the federal and provincial parliamentary systems is that the provinces do not have upper houses like the Senate. They have only one elected house, the Legislative Assembly. Before Confederation, the colonies did have appointed upper houses known as Legislative Councils. The provinces have now abolished them. There is nothing to suggest that the provinces have suffered as a result. Provincial governments have found other ways to reward the party faithful.

The office of Lieutenant Governor provides another difference between the provincial and federal parliamentary systems. The Lieutenant Governors and the Governor General both represent the Crown and perform similar tasks. But the Lieutenant Governors are appointed by the Governor General

Following the court decision that a woman was a "person" and could be appointed to the Senate, the Department of Justice concluded that there were no legal obstacles to a woman as Lieutenant Governor. However, it was not until 1974 that Pauline McGibbon was appointed as the first woman Lieutenant Governor. Here Lieutenant Governor McGibbon arrives at Queen's Park to open the 1981 session of the Ontario Legislative Assembly.

on the advice of the prime minister of Canada. They are not appointed on the advice of the provincial premiers. The prime minister may consult a provincial premier on an appointment, but there is no need to do so. The appointment often goes to a deserving member of the federal party in power. It may even go to someone who had been opposed to the party now in power in the province.

Originally, the Lieutenant Governors were meant to act as agents or servants of the federal government. This role became much less important as the provinces became more important. Today, no one thinks of the Lieutenant Governor as a federal officer. Yet, as recently as 1937, the federal government instructed Alberta's Lieutenant Governor to reserve bills for Ottawa's consideration. This meant that the Lieutenant Governor would not sign the bills into law until the federal government had examined and approved them. This power to reserve is now looked upon as obsolete or out of date.

WHAT DO THE PROVINCIAL GOVERNMENTS DO?

The chart on page 147 indicates some of the many activities of provincial governments. The organization and role of the government departments or ministries differ from province to province. Prince Edward Island has only ten ministers, while Alberta, Quebec, and Ontario have more than twenty. The other provinces have between fifteen and twenty. In some of the smaller provinces, one cabinet minister is in charge of several departments. Provincial departments also differ because of the nature of the provincial economies. All of the Atlantic provinces have ministries of fisheries. British Columbia has a minister of forests. Ontario includes the management of its fish and forest resources in a broad ministry of natural resources.

The pie graphs on page 150 show where the provinces get their money and what they spend it on. Taxes on personal incomes is one of the largest sources of provincial income. The federal government collects these taxes for all provinces except Quebec. Of the taxes collected for them, each province gets back a percentage, to which they then add their own provincial taxes. Alberta and Saskatchewan depend less on income taxes than the other provinces. Over half of Alberta's income and one quarter of Saskatchewan's comes from natural resources, mainly oil and gas. Only one per cent of Ontario's income comes from taxes on natural resources. Expenditures on health and education rank first and second in all

Provincial Income and Expenditure

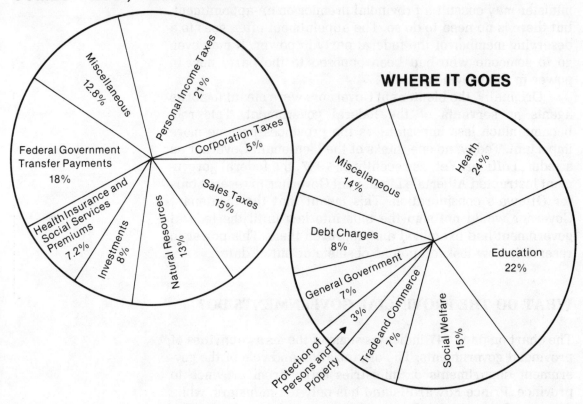

WHERE PROVINCIAL MONEY COMES FROM, ALL PROVINCES

- Miscellaneous 12.8%
- Personal Income Taxes 21%
- Corporation Taxes 5%
- Federal Government Transfer Payments 18%
- Sales Taxes 15%
- Health Insurance and Social Services Premiums 7.2%
- Investments 8%
- Natural Resources 13%

WHERE IT GOES

- Miscellaneous 14%
- Health 24%
- Debt Charges 8%
- Education 22%
- General Government 7%
- Protection of Persons and Property 3%
- Trade and Commerce 7%
- Social Welfare 15%

provinces except British Columbia. In that province, welfare costs were slightly higher in 1981 than were the costs of education.

Local Government

The provincial governments do not look after all of their responsibilities directly. Each province has created a system of local governments and local boards or agencies, and has given them power to deal with important local matters. The local governments are not independent of the provincial governments. They are created by provincial law and get all their authority from provincial governments. At any time, the provinces may change the rules or the system.

It is not easy to describe local government because each province has its own system. Most provinces use such names as village, town, city, county, and metropolitan area. But the organization of local governments and the responsibilities given to them by various provinces are very different. Provincial departments of municipal affairs or local government headquarters are the best sources of local government information.

WHY HAVE LOCAL GOVERNMENT?

A century ago it was not hard to understand why local governments existed. People in a certain area elected them to look after such local matters as roads, schools, the water supply if there was one, police and fire protection, and other local needs that might need attention. They raised their own taxes and borrowed money to provide for roads, sewers, and water supply. In a country of small and scattered villages and towns, such a system worked reasonably well. At the time of Confederation, for example, only one Canadian in six lived in the 21 urban communities that contained more than 5000 people.

Urban Growth

Canada today is a very different country. Only one Canadian in five lives outside the 1046 urban areas of more than 1000 people. Many of these live in the shadows of sprawling towns and cities. The rise of industry and the growth of the city, which we call *urbanization*, dramatically changed the nature of local government. A water and sewage system good enough for a small town could not begin to meet the needs of a growing city. Cities also had much greater need for police and fire protection. New inventions such as electricity, streetcars, and buses provided new services for city dwellers. But they also created new problems. And while the new factories provided jobs, they also reduced the quality of life for those who lived near them.

After the Second World War, cities began to spread out beyond their former boundaries. Farmlands became residential suburbs or the location for new industries. Expressways linked the larger cities and swept through or around towns and villages. As the cities expanded, there was a need for larger and better hospitals and schools. Individual towns and villages could no longer plan for their own futures because they no longer lived in isolation.

New Responsibilities

As a result of these developments, the range of government activities increased greatly. We have seen that many of the new activities, such as health and welfare, aid to the needy, housing, and cultural and recreational facilities, came within the powers of the provincial governments. The provinces, therefore, had to decide how best to meet the new needs.

The provinces dealt with each new problem as it came up. Tiny Prince Edward Island, with a population smaller than many cities, found that it could deal with many local matters from the provincial capital. Ontario, with a large population and enormous territory, decided that many services should be provided at the local level. This would be done either through elected local governments and school boards, or through local bodies or agencies created for a particular purpose. The latter would include, for example, health units, library boards, and police commissions.

Local Responsibilities

Today, in general, the following services are handled at the local level.

Education:	Elementary and secondary schools
Culture and Recreation:	Parks, swimming pools and ice rinks, libraries, art galleries
Health and Welfare:	Public health services, ambulances, welfare administration
Housing:	Homes for the aged, low rental housing, building permits and standards
Land Use:	Planning and zoning
Protection:	Police, fire, animal control, building and construction, emergency measures
Transportation:	Public transit, streets and roads, traffic control
Utilities:	Water, collection and disposal of garbage and sewage, distribution of electricity

Although there are differences among the provinces and even within a province, there are three main ways in which these local services are provided and paid for in addition to services provided directly by the province.

1. The province sets the standards, provides the funds, and sets up a *special agency, such as a hospital board, to administer the service.*

2. The province sets the standards, provides some or all of the funds, and *allows the local government to administer the service under provincial control.*

3. The local government *has complete responsibility for running the service and providing the funds.*

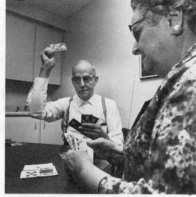

LOCAL RESPONSIBILITIES

*(Top left) Education
(Top right) Senior Citizens*

*(Middle left) Protection
(Middle) Health
(Middle right) Utilities*

Planning and Zoning

Transportation

Today in Ontario, for example, half of the local services fall within the first category. One quarter fall within the second. Even in such areas as parks, streets, sidewalks and water distribution, where the local government has direct control, the province still has a voice. For the province controls the local government's borrowing of money, land use planning, and environmental policy. From one end of the country to the other, the most frequent complaint of local governments is that they have little freedom to make independent decisions on most important matters.

HOW ARE LOCAL GOVERNMENTS ORGANIZED?

The basic unit of local government is the *municipality*. It may be a township, village, town, or city. Municipalities may range in population from a few hundred to hundreds of thousands. Their responsibilities vary according to their size and the way in which each province has distributed responsibilities. In many provinces, local municipalities are grouped into larger units for some purposes. Larger units include districts, counties, regions, or, in the case of some of the large cities, metropolitan governments. It is not possible to examine all ten provinces, but Ontario and British Columbia provide two interesting examples.

WHERE MUNICIPAL MONEY COMES FROM

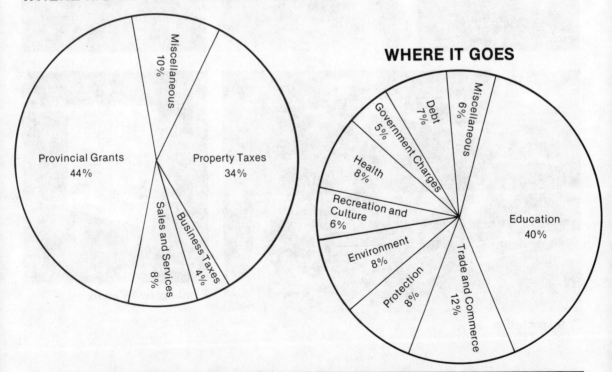

WHERE IT GOES

In Ontario there are 800 local governments of at least nine different types. There are, as well, more than 2000 local bodies of one kind or another. Nothing shows more clearly the difficulty in understanding local government in Canada today!

Ontario has what is called a two-level or "two-tier" system of local government. The bottom tier is the local municipality. This may be a city, town, village or township. A township is the only rural municipality and must have a population of 1000 before it can be incorporated. A village has between 500 and 2000 people, and a town between 2000 and 15 000. A city must have more than 15 000 people. The government of a city or town is headed by a mayor who is elected by all of the voters. There are also aldermen who are elected by the voters in each ward or district of a city or town. Villages and townships elect a reeve as head of the government, and a number of councillors.

All of these units, *except the city*, form part of a larger unit called a *county*. The county is the second tier of local government. Today, there are 27 counties in Ontario. County governments are not elected directly by the voters but are made up of the mayors and reeves of all the local municipalities, except the cities, in the county. One mayor or reeve is elected as warden to head the county council.

Until the 1950s, this was the system of local government that existed throughout southern Ontario. After the Second World War, the system began to break down. It did so for three main reasons. First, there was a rapid growth of urban areas in the province. Almost two thirds of the people now lived in cities. Yet the cities were not part of the two-level system of local government. Second, as a result of the rapidly growing urban areas, the boundaries of the counties no longer served to mark off distinct economic or social units. Finally, the expansion of government activities made it necessary to reorganize educational, health and welfare, and protection and transportation services.

Politicians first tackled the problem raised by these changes in what is now Metropolitan Toronto. By 1950, there were almost half a million people living in the twelve municipalities that bordered on the city of Toronto. Outside the city itself, there were 32 private transportation systems. Each one of the twelve municipalities had its own water and sewage systems. Some of these systems were actually dangerous to public health because the municipalities did not have access to good water and lacked safe sewage disposal places. There was no common planning for roads, parks, or industrial development. As the population of the area soared, the situation became impossible.

METROPOLITAN TORONTO: RESPONSIBILITIES OF
LOCAL GOVERNMENTS AND OF THE METRO GOVERNMENT

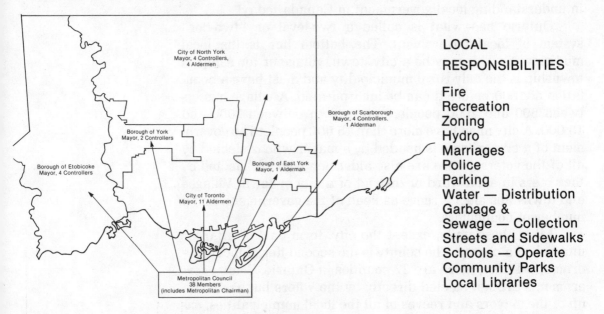

LOCAL
RESPONSIBILITIES

Fire
Recreation
Zoning
Hydro
Marriages
Police
Parking
Water — Distribution
Garbage &
Sewage — Collection
Streets and Sidewalks
Schools — Operate
Community Parks
Local Libraries

City of North York
Mayor, 4 Controllers,
4 Aldermen

Borough of Scarborough
Mayor, 4 Controllers.
1 Alderman

Borough of York
Mayor, 2 Controllers

Borough of East York
Mayor, 1 Alderman

Borough of Etobicoke
Mayor, 4 Controllers

City of Toronto
Mayor, 11 Aldermen

Metropolitan Council
38 Members
(includes Metropolitan Chairman)

METRO RESPONSIBILITIES

Transit (TTC)	Water — Supply	Schools — Finance
Police	Garbage &	Regional Parks &
Ambulance	Sewage — Disposal	Golf Courses
Borrowing	Major Roads and	Welfare
Business Licences	Expressways	Emergency

In 1953, the provincial government responded to the problem by creating Metropolitan Toronto. Metropolitan Toronto is like a miniature federation. Each of the thirteen local municipalities, including the city of Toronto, was left with certain powers. A new higher level of government was set up and given powers over matters that applied to the entire metropolitan area. In 1968, the number of municipalities in Metro Toronto was reduced from thirteen to the present number of six.

The metropolitan experiment proved to be very successful. Despite many problems, Metro Toronto became a model for many other cities in Canada and the United States. The present responsibilities of the local governments and the Metro government are shown on the diagram above.

The Toronto region was not the only part of Ontario to grow rapidly. The provincial population soared from 4.5 million in 1951 to 6.2 million in 1961 and 7.7 million in 1971. One effect of this growth was to change completely the area around Toronto, Hamilton, Ottawa, Windsor, Kitchener-Waterloo, and on the Niagara peninsula. To deal with these changes, the provincial government, beginning in the 1960s, created eleven new regional governments along the lines of Metropolitan Toronto. The new regional governments included one or more counties and all of the cities within those counties. The new upper level of regional government was given responsibility for regional planning, roads, water supply and sewage disposal, public transit, and parks and welfare services. In addition, some of the local municipalities were joined together as larger units. For example, the city of Cambridge was formed from Galt, Hespeler, and Preston. Cambridge is now in the Regional Municipality of Waterloo.

WHERE EACH TAX DOLLAR GOES

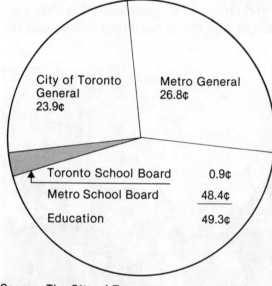

Source: The City of Toronto

An Example

In 1982, a typical single-family home in the City of Toronto, assessed at $5,000 will pay $1,122 in taxes. Of this $1,122, $554 will go to education, $268 to the City and $300 to Metro.

The $554 for education is divided between elementary and secondary schools.

The City uses $268 to pay for the expenses of the fire department, roads, sidewalks, garbage collection, parks, public health, planning, building inspections, libraries, recreation services and debt charges from funding such capital projects as sewer construction.

The kind of services provided by the $300 allocated to Metro includes the police, social services and child welfare, major roads and traffic, garbage disposal, the reference library, regional parks, the zoo and ambulance services.

The local municipalities within the regional governments kept many of their former powers. These usually included responsibility for local roads, garbage collection, recreational facilities, and other community services. Including Metropolitan Toronto, these regional governments now contain almost two thirds of the population of the province of Ontario.

In sparsely settled northern Ontario, the organization of local government is different from that of the more populous south. Local municipalities in the north are grouped within districts. Each district has an association to discuss common problems and sometimes to take common action. In the *far* north, there are no local governments. The provincial government provides local services directly.

British Columbia

British Columbia is a province of mountains and rivers that set natural barriers between villages, towns, and cities. Much of the province is still unsettled, and is organized into districts that provide some local services under the supervision of the provincial government.

As in Ontario, the postwar boom caused enormous growth in the Pacific province. The growth was most marked around the city of Vancouver, on Vancouver Island, and in the lumbering, agricultural and mining centres of the interior. The population of British Columbia increased from 1.165 million in 1951 to 2.466 million in 1977. By 1981, it had reached 2.716 million. During the same period, Greater Vancouver jumped from 345 000 to 1 200 000. Improved road transportation helped to knit together some of the province's towns and cities, such as those in the lower mainland around Vancouver and those along the east coast of Vancouver Island. Better highways also brought rural areas and many small communities within easy reach of the larger towns and cities scattered throughout the province.

The first meeting of Vancouver City Council, 1886

As in Ontario, it became both desirable and possible to create larger municipal units to provide many modern services to the growing urban and rural population. In 1946, the provincial government reorganized hundreds of small local school boards into district boards. The government also created special boards to provide water and sewage services over larger areas. Finally, in 1965, the provincial government set up 28 regional districts that took in all of the province except the northwest. Within each district there was a regional board made up of representatives of each of the municipalities within the district. In this respect, the regional boards were similar to the county councils in Ontario.

At first, the regional boards had little power. Local municipalities were free to opt in or out of many regional services. But as time passed, the boards' responsibilities grew. Today the regional boards are responsible for hospital services, regional planning, the development of some community services, and the provision of some water supply and sewage disposal systems. The most important regional district is that of Greater Vancouver where almost half of the provincial population lives.

Local municipalities in British Columbia often opposed the introduction of the regional district just as the county councils did in Ontario. In both provinces, the local municipalities objected to a loss of much of their power. In both British Columbia and Ontario, the regional government approach is an experiment in trying to modernize local government without destroying the older systems.

VOTING STRENGTH OF GREATER VANCOUVER REGIONAL DISTRICT MEMBERS

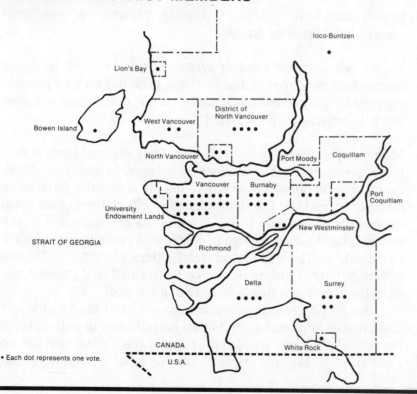

• Each dot represents one vote.

The Greater Vancouver Regional District is composed of 17 communities. Each community elects members to the board of the district. The board is responsible for regional planning, regional hospital planning, parks, water supply and sewage disposal, pollution control, and housing. Before the board takes over responsibility for some area, two thirds of the members representing at least two thirds of the population must approve.

Other provinces faced with the same problems as Ontario and British Columbia generally have also moved to larger units of local government in order to provide improved services for their people. But no province claims to have discovered a magic solution to the difficult problems of local government.

Municipal Finance

One of the major problems everywhere in Canada is how to pay for local services. In general, across the country, about 40% of local government income comes from the provincial governments. In British Columbia, the amount is only 28%, while in Prince Edward Island, it reaches 80%. Local governments themselves must raise the rest. Almost 60% of this money comes from taxes on such property as homes, apartments, and businesses. For the home owner in particular, these taxes have become a very heavy burden. As a result, hard-pressed local governments repeatedly demand that provincial and federal governments provide more funds, or that they give the local governments a share in the personal income tax that everyone must pay. To date, they have not been successful.

LOCAL GOVERNMENT: THE CRADLE OF DEMOCRACY?

John Stuart Mill, a brilliant English philosopher who lived about a century ago, wrote:

We do not learn to read or write, to ride or swim by being merely told how to do it, but by doing it; so it is only by practising popular government on a limited scale, that people will ever learn to exercise it on a larger.

Many people have agreed with Mill. They maintain that it is in local government that citizens can learn to practise democracy. For in local government people can take part more directly in making the decisions that affect them. Our local community is familiar to us. We can understand most of the issues. The children who go to school and cross the streets are our children. The police and fire fighters protect us. We can talk to our local alderman, or go to city hall and present our case for a new park or a new swimming pool.

But do Canadians practise democracy at the local level? The answer, unfortunately, is that most do not. In national and provincial elections more than 70% of the voters turn out on election day. But the turnout for all local elections across

Canada for the last twenty years has been about 30%. In the 1974 elections in Metro Toronto only 25% voted in the Borough of Scarborough and 31% in the city of Toronto itself. In Ontario's Essex County in the same year, over one third of all the seats in the town and village councils and one half the seats on the school boards were not even contested.

How can we explain this lack of interest in local government?

Is it because political parties do not usually contest local elections and as a result there is less interest and enthusiasm than during national or provincial elections?

Is it because the matters local governments deal with seem boring?

Is it because the mass media concentrates on the more exciting issues facing the country or the world?

Is it because we just cannot be bothered unless an issue affects us very directly, such as a notice that our property taxes have been doubled or that an expressway is planned that will run through our immediate neighbourhood?

Whatever the reason, the health of our local governments is one of the matters we must be concerned with when we ask How are we governed?

STUDY GUIDE

Getting the Facts

1. Define each of the following: Lieutenant Governor, local government, central government, pie graph, urbanization, utilities, zoning, building permit, building standards, municipality, *two-tier* system of government, incorporated, mayor, alderman, reeve, councillor, ward, county, region.
2. What does the pie graph on page 150 reveal about provincial spending?
3. In what ways have the responsibilities of local governments increased?
4. Why have provincial governments reorganized their systems of local governments in recent years?

Using the Facts

1. Do you believe that the provincial governments give the local governments too little responsibility and freedom of action?
2. Do you agree with John Stuart Mill that local government should be "the cradle of democracy"? Why do most people seem to be indifferent?
3. Do you believe that property owners should carry so much of the burden of paying for local government?

Research Projects

1. Draw a tourist map for your municipality (local government). On this map locate the following: municipal offices, firehall, local police station, local museums, libraries, schools, etc. It is likely that your municipality has a special history that should be promoted. Perhaps there is a crest or coat of arms that highlights this history and that might provide an attractive focus for tourists. Statistical data concerning population, occupations, and taxation could also be included in table form. Most municipalities have special events that attract tourists. Does yours?
2. When annual taxes are collected, most municipalities publish a pie graph explaining where the money is spent. See if you can discover this information for your municipality and design a pamphlet that would make taxation more acceptable to taxpayers.
3. Would John Stuart Mill have admired your municipality? Suggest three ways that your local government tries to encourage community involvement.
4. Is voter turnout for municipal elections in your community as low as elsewhere in Canada? What explains the relatively low turnout in local elections? In answering this question interview some of your local elected officials on this subject.

5. A Toronto city dump in 1914. The ninth by-law passed after York became the City of Toronto in 1834 read:

   It shall be the duty of the Street Surveyor from the first day of May to the first day of September, in every year, to cause a cart to pass once in every day except Sundays through all the streets in the City and the drivers of such carts shall give notice of their approach by ringing a hand-bell and shall receive all vegetables, ashes, offalls, or garbage which shall be delivered at such carts under a penalty of twenty-five shillings for every neglect or refusal.

   From your local town or city records find out when your local government assumed responsibility for the tasks listed on page 152.

Chapter 9
WHAT IS
THE RULE OF LAW?

What Is the Rule of Law?

How Does the Canada Act, 1982, Protect Our Freedom?

Canadian Charter of Rights and Freedoms
Guarantee of Rights and Freedoms
Fundamental Freedoms
Democratic Rights
Mobility Rights
Legal Rights
Equality Rights
Official Languages of Canada
Minority Language Educational Rights
Enforcement
General
Application of Charter

The Judiciary
Criminal and Civil Law
The Courts
The Judges

The majesty of the law: the Supreme Court of Canada

The daily presence of the law

Two thousand years ago, a Roman named Cicero wrote: "We are all slaves of the law that we may be free." Cicero put together two opposite ideas — slavery and freedom — to draw attention to the importance of the point he was making. His words are as true in Canada today as they were in ancient Rome. And they contain the single most important idea about our whole system of government.

Cicero was really saying two things. The first is that the law is the master and we, all of us, are under the control of and must obey the master. The second is that we accept this domination by the law willingly so that we may enjoy the greatest possible amount of freedom. These two ideas are the basis of democratic, parliamentary government in Canada. They include a number of other ideas that are also important in helping to answer the basic question of this book, "How are we governed?" We usually sum up all of these ideas in the phrase, "the rule of law."

WHAT IS THE RULE OF LAW?

Like some of the other most important words in the English language "law" is very short. A one-syllable, three-letter word we use all the time. Perhaps because it is so familiar, we sometimes use it carelessly and confuse its real meaning. For example, we sometimes use the expression "the Law" when talking about the police officer patrolling a beat or investigating a crime. And we are all familiar with the "lawman" of the western movie. The police, however, are not the law. Their job is to see that the law is obeyed in order "that we may be free." They are as much "slaves of the law" as the rest of us.

When we speak of "the rule of law," we do not mean the police. We are thinking about that basic principle or idea on which our system of government rests. The rule of law means:

1. that no one, regardless of position or power, is excused from obeying the law.

2. that everyone is equal in the eyes of the law. The law must be the same for people of all races and beliefs, for male and female, rich and poor.

3. that it is the law that states what power the government has over us and what freedoms we have under that government. This means that the government gets its authority to rule from the law. It cannot govern in defiance of the law.

The police may arrest someone suspected of breaking the law. But from that moment on, our legal system is designed to protect those arrested unless they can be found guilty in a fair and honest trial.

4. that the freedom of any individual can be limited only by those we have elected and only in ways that have been agreed on, such as those for passing a bill in Parliament. In our democratic system, the law restricts what the government can do and the way it can do it. In a dictatorship, what the dictator or ruler wants to do has the force of law.

5. that it is the law that protects our lives and our property from one another's anger or greed.

As we think about the broad meaning of the rule of law in Canada, it becomes clear that almost everything we talk about in *How Are We Governed?* is included. Elections, Parliament, Cabinet, and our federal system are all part of the rule of law in Canada. Together they lay down the rules that the government must follow in imposing its will on us or, simply, in governing.

Most of the time we do not think in broad terms about the rule of law. We think of the laws themselves. In a democracy, *laws* are the rules and regulations that the people, through their elected representatives, have agreed upon to make it possible to live in peace and order. Every law limits in some way what a person may do. At the same time, every law protects an individual's freedom. For example, speed limits set the speeds at which everyone may drive so that we may all drive in greater safety. There are also laws that prevent business firms from selling impure foods or contractors from building unsafe buildings. Such laws are made by the Parliament of Canada, provincial legislatures, or by municipal governments to which the provincial governments have given this power.

HOW DOES THE CANADA ACT, 1982, PROTECT OUR FREEDOM?

We have said that our governments pass laws that limit our freedom to do anything we might wish in order to serve the interest of the country as a whole. However, Canadians also believe that there are some rights and freedoms that the government must not only protect, but that the government cannot limit, except, perhaps, in the case of a national emergency such as a war. These are rights and freedoms that we believe are essential if we are to have a true democracy. Although our federal and provincial governments have passed laws to protect such rights and freedoms, the laws have not always done so. And the governments that passed the laws could also change them if they wished. At times in Canada's past, governments have not respected our freedoms or accepted limits on their own power.

To prevent such abuses and to protect our democratic freedoms, many Canadians urged that there be a statement of these rights that all governments would accept and enforce, and that they could not easily change. After years of discussion and debate, Prime Minister Trudeau and the provincial premiers agreed to make certain rights and freedoms a basic part of the law of the Canadian nation. The result was the *Canadian Charter of Rights and Freedoms.* The Charter is an essential part of Canada's new constitution, the Canada Act of 1982.

The language of the Charter is not easy to understand. And no one is completely sure what the various rights and freedoms will mean in practice. As with all laws, the courts will have to decide exactly what rights and freedoms Canadians have. Already, many lawyers have tried to indicate what the various sections of the Charter may mean. In the next section, we shall also make an attempt to suggest the meaning and importance of the clauses of the Charter.

CANADIAN CHARTER OF RIGHTS AND FREEDOMS

Whereas Canada is founded upon principles that recognize the supremacy of God and the rule of law:

GUARANTEE OF RIGHTS AND FREEDOMS

1. The *Canadian Charter of Rights and Freedoms* guarantees the rights and freedoms set out in it subject only to such reasonable limits prescribed by law as can be demonstrably justified in a free and democratic society.

---

1. This has been called the "common sense" clause. Actually, it is intended to give governments the power to limit our freedoms as long as they can justify the limitation as "reasonable." Clearly, a person cannot use the right of freedom of expression to make false accusations against others; the law of libel sets limits on that freedom. But what is "reasonable?" What limitations are justifiable in a democracy? Parliament will debate such questions and finally the courts will decide.

FUNDAMENTAL FREEDOMS

2. Everyone has the following fundamental freedoms:
(a) freedom of conscience and religion;
(b) freedom of thought, belief, opinion and expression, including freedom of the press and other media of communication;
(c) Freedom of peaceful assembly; and
(d) freedom of association.

---

2. Most Canadians have always looked on these freedoms as vital to the working of our democracy. There are some people, however, who think that the freedoms are too broad. Freedom of expression, for example, might mean that there was no way to prevent publication of material that attacked minority groups, or that offended good taste or decency. Others suggest that the guarantee of freedom of assembly might make it difficult to control demonstrations and prevent riots. For these reasons, the provincial governments insisted that this section of the Charter come within the provisions of Section 33, which we will discuss later.

DEMOCRATIC RIGHTS

3. Every citizen of Canada has the right to vote in an election of members of the House of Commons or of a legislative assembly and to be qualified for membership therein.

4. (1) No House of Commons and no legislative assembly shall continue for longer than five years from the date fixed for the return of the writs at a general election of its members.

(2) In time of real or apprehended war, invasion or insurrection, a House of Commons may be continued by Parliament and a legislative assembly may be continued by the legislature beyond five years if such continuation is not opposed by the votes of more than one-third of the members of the House of Commons or the legislative assembly, as the case may be.

5. There shall be a sitting of Parliament and of each legislature at least once every twelve months.

3-5. Most Canadians have long taken these democratic rights for granted. The British North America Act provided for annual sessions of Parliament and of the provincial legislatures. The act also limited the life of the House of Commons and the provincial assemblies to five years. During the First World War, Parliament did extend its life. This would still be possible, but only if no more than one third of the members were opposed. During wartime, Section 3 of the Charter probably would prevent governments from taking away the vote of naturalized citizens who came from an enemy country, as the federal government did from naturalized Canadians of German origin during the 1917 wartime election. It would also stop any government from denying the right to vote to any minority group, as was the case with citizens of Asian origin and some Native peoples until after the Second World War.

MOBILITY RIGHTS

6. (1) Every citizen of Canada has the right to enter, remain in and leave Canada.

(2) Every citizen of Canada and every person who has the status of a permanent resident of Canada has the right
  (a) to move to and take up residence in any province; and
  (b) to pursue the gaining of a livelihood in any province.

(3) The rights specified in subsection (2) are subject to
  (a) any laws or practices of general application in force in a province other than those that discriminate among persons primarily on the basis of province of present or previous residence; and
  (b) any laws providing for reasonable residency requirements as a qualification for the receipt of publicly provided social services.

(4) Subsections (2) and (3) do not preclude any law, program or activity that has as its object the amelioration in a province of conditions of individuals in that province who are socially or economically disadvantaged if the rate of employment in that province is below the rate of employment in Canada.

6. In recent years, some provinces have placed limitations on the right of other Canadians to come to those provinces to work. This section puts an end to such practices. Subsection (4), however, makes it possible for provinces with high unemployment to help their own residents first. Provinces still have the right to limit non-residents from owning property. Prince Edward Island was concerned about non-residents buying up waterfront property, and Saskatchewan was determined to prevent outsiders from buying up farms.

LEGAL RIGHTS

7. Everyone has the right to life, liberty and security of the person and the right not to be deprived thereof except in accordance with the principles of fundamental justice.

7. This clause is likely to be very difficult to interpret. Exactly what is meant by "the right to life?" When does life begin? What is meant by "principles of fundamental justice?" This clause is most likely to involve the courts in issues of abortion and the death penalty.

8. Everyone has the right to be secure against unreasonable search or seizure.

9. Everyone has the right not to be arbitrarily detained or imprisoned.

10. Everyone has the right on arrest or detention
(a) to be informed promptly of the reasons therefor;
(b) to retain and instruct counsel without delay and to be informed of that right; and
(c) to have the validity of the detention determined by way of *habeas corpus* and to be released if the detention is not lawful.

8-10. The Canadian Criminal Code includes similar sections, although the right *to be informed* of the right to secure a lawyer is a new provision. But in the new constitution, it will be up to the judges in our courts to decide just what is meant by such phrases as "unreasonable search," "arbitrarily imprisoned," or "informed promptly." Some police officers believe that these clauses could seriously interfere with their efforts to find and arrest criminals. They point out that it is often impossible to state exactly or promptly what the charge might or should be when they arrest a suspected criminal. Other critics fear that the clauses may give the police too much power. What is reasonable or arbitrary or prompt in the opinion of one judge may be quite different to another.

11. Any person charged with an offence has the right
(a) to be informed without unreasonable delay of the specific offence;
(b) to be tried within a reasonable time;
(c) not to be compelled to be a witness in proceedings against that person in respect of the offence;
(d) to be presumed innocent until proven guilty according to law in a fair and public hearing by an independent and impartial tribunal;
(e) not to be denied reasonable bail without just cause;
(f) except in the case of an offence under military law tried before a military tribunal, to the benefit of trial by jury where the maximum punishment for the offence is imprisonment for five years or a more severe punishment;
(g) not to be found guilty on account of any act or omission unless, at the time of the act or omission, it constituted an offence under Canadian international law or was criminal according to the general principles of law recognized by the community of nations;
(h) if finally acquitted of the offence, not to be tried for it again and, if finally found guilty and punished for the offence, not to be tried or punished for it again; and
(i) if found guilty of the offence and if the punishment for the offence has been varied between the time of commission and the time of sentencing, to the benefit of the lesser punishment.

11. This clause lists some of the fundamental rights for anyone charged with committing a crime. All those accused have the right to know the charges against them and the right to a speedy trial. They cannot be forced to give evidence against themselves. Every accused person is considered to be innocent until found guilty by a judge or, if the offence carries a severe penalty, by a jury. Subsection (g) could prevent governments from suddenly deciding that membership in a particular organization is a crime. In 1970, for example, the federal government made membership in the Front de libération du Québec illegal, and then arrested those who had joined that organization before it was a crime to do so.

> **12.** Everyone has the right not to be subjected to any cruel and unusual treatment or punishment.

12. Some people believe that defence lawyers will try to use this section to challenge sentences handed down in court. Others fear, or hope, that "cruel and unusual" may lead to another debate on capital punishment. Will long periods of solitary confinement be regarded as a cruel punishment?

> **13.** A witness who testifies in any proceedings has the right not to have any incriminating evidence so given used to incriminate that witness in any other proceedings, except in a prosecution for perjury or for the giving of contradictory evidence.

13. This section broadens existing guarantees. It means that if Mr. Jones is charged with the robbery of a bank in Toronto, he can defend himself successfully by proving that at the time of the Toronto robbery he was, in fact, robbing a store in Winnipeg. The police may not then charge him with robbing the store in Winnipeg, unless they can find other evidence that he had done so.

> **14.** A party or witness in any proceedings who does not understand or speak the language in which the proceedings are conducted or who is deaf has the right to the assistance of an interpreter.

14. The meaning of Section 14 is clear. It is a long-overdue guarantee for those whose innocence might not be proved because they cannot understand or speak English or French.

EQUALITY RIGHTS

15. (1) Every individual is equal before and under the law and has the right to the equal protection and equal benefit of the law without discrimination and, in particular, without discrimination based on race, national or ethnic origin, colour, religion, sex, age or mental or physical disability.
(2) Subsection (1) does not preclude any law, program or activity that has as its object the amelioration of conditions of disadvantaged individuals or groups including those that are disadvantaged because of race, national or ethnic origin, colour, religion, sex, age or mental or physical disability.

15. There was general agreement that the constitution should guarantee legal equality regardless of a person's race, national or ethnic origin, colour, and religion. But some premiers. questioned the wisdom of including sex, age, and mental or physical disability. Should women serve as combat soldiers? Is compulsory retirement legal? Will public buildings and transportation vehicles have to be rebuilt to accommodate wheelchairs? Will paper money have to be reprinted so that the blind can distinguish between bills of different denominations? The possible consequences of Section 15 (1) seemed so great that the provinces included it in Section 33 of the Charter. In addition, the clause was not to come into effect until 1985 (Section 32 (2)). Subsection (2) means that the government may give favoured treatment to the disadvantaged. In other words, some people are permitted to be more "equal" than others.

OFFICIAL LANGUAGES OF CANADA

Sections 16-19 also apply to New Brunswick. New Brunswick was the only province to become officially bilingual under the constitution.

---

16. (1) English and French are the official languages of Canada and have equality of status and equal rights and privileges as to their use in all institutions of the Parliament and government of Canada.

(3) Nothing in this Charter limits the authority of Parliament or a legislature to advance the equality of status or use of English and French.

17. (1) Everyone has the right to use English or French in any debates and other proceedings of Parliament.

18. (1) The statutes, records and journals of Parliament shall be printed and published in English and French and both language versions are equally authoritative.

19. (1) Either English or French may be used by any person in, or in any pleading in or process issuing from, any court established by Parliament.

20. (1) Any member of the public in Canada has the right to communicate with, and to receive available services from, any head or central office of an institution of the Parliament or government of Canada in English or French, and has the same right with respect to any other office of any such institution where

(a) there is a significant demand for communications with and services from that office in such language; or

(b) due to the nature of the office, it is reasonable that communications with and services from that office be available in both English and French.

16-20. These sections place in the Canadian constitution the provisions of the Official Languages Act of 1969. However, Section 20 broadens the obligation of the federal government to provide services in French or English. It will be up to the courts to decide what is a "significant demand," or whether it is "reasonable" that customers at a post office in Toronto, Vancouver, Halifax, or Chicoutimi may use either French or English.

---

21. Nothing in sections 16 to 20 abrogates or derogates from any right, privilege or obligation with respect to the English and French languages, or either of them, that exists or is continued by virtue of any other provision of the Constitution of Canada.

21. This section means that Sections 16-20 in no way limit the provisions of the British North America Act of 1867 (Section 133) or the Manitoba Act of 1870. These two acts permit the use of both English and French in the legislatures and courts of Quebec and Manitoba. Bill 101, passed in 1977 by Quebec's National Assembly, had abolished the use of English in the Assembly. However, the Supreme Court of Canada ruled in 1981 that the Quebec government did not have the power to do so because of Section 133 of the British North America Act.

22. Nothing in sections 16 to 20 abrogates or derogates from any legal or customary right or privilege acquired or enjoyed either before or after the coming into force of this Charter with respect to any language that is not English or French.

22. This section is meant to assure Native peoples that they will be able to continue to use their own languages in court cases and on radio and television.

MINORITY LANGUAGE EDUCATIONAL RIGHTS

23. (1) Citizens of Canada

(a) whose first language learned and still understood is that of the English or French linguistic minority population of the province in which they reside, or

(b) who have received their primary school instruction in Canada in English or French and reside in a province where the language in which they received that instruction is the language of the English or French linguistic minority population of the province,

have the right to have their children receive primary and secondary school instruction in that language in that province.

(2) Citizens of Canada of whom any child has received or is receiving primary or secondary school instruction in English or French in Canada, have the right to have all their children receive primary and secondary school instruction in the same language.

(3) The right of citizens of Canada under subsections (1) and (2) to have their children receive primary and secondary instruction in the language of the English or French linguistic minority population of a province

(a) applies wherever in the province the number of children of citizens who have such a right is sufficient to warrant the provision to them out of public funds of minority language instruction; and

(b) includes, where the number of those children so warrants, the right to have them receive that instruction in minority language educational facilities provided out of public funds.

23. On pages 133-41, we explained why this section on minority language educational rights was very difficult to work out. The final version is not easy to understand. What does it guarantee? The section provides guarantees only for Canadian citizens. Children of immigrants do not have freedom to choose their language of instruction. Thus, the section does not affect Quebec's determination to educate immigrant children in French. There are even limits on the freedom of choice for the children of Canadian citizens. Only those citizens who

(a) first learned either French or English

(b) who attended a French or English primary school and who now live in a province where the language in which

they were taught is that of the minority of the population (English in Quebec and French in the other provinces)
(c) have already begun educating one child in French or English,

have freedom to choose the language in which their children will be educated. It would appear that many new Canadians will have freedom of choice only under (c).

Although Section 23 sets out minority language educational rights, the provinces have to provide minority language schools only where there are enough students to justify such schools. But what is a sufficient number of students? Saskatchewan might decide that ten students in a community are enough, while British Columbia might set the number at fifty. It is likely that the courts will be asked to decide. And the decision is likely to be more a political than a legal one.

Finally, since Quebec was completely opposed to the guarantees, Section 59 of the Canada Act provided that Section 23 (1(a)) would come into effect in Quebec only when the government of Quebec agreed.

For all of these reasons, many Canadians believe that while Section 23 is an admirable statement of principles, it will not have much immediate effect.

ENFORCEMENT

24. (1) Anyone whose rights or freedoms, as guaranteed by this Charter, have been infringed or denied may apply to a court of competent jurisdiction to obtain such remedy as the court considers appropriate and just in the circumstances.
(2) Where, in proceedings under subsection (1), a court concludes that evidence was obtained in a manner that infringed or denied any rights or freedoms guaranteed by this Charter, the evidence shall be excluded if it is established that, having regard to all the circumstances, the admission of it in the proceedings would bring the administration of justice into disrepute.

---

24. Those responsible for keeping law and order have opposed this section. They agree that the courts must protect those whose rights and freedoms have been denied. But they believe that this clause will shelter the guilty, and that defence lawyers will always try to prove that the police denied the accused the legal rights guaranteed in Sections 7 to 14. The police will then be sued. This possibility, say opponents of this section, will make the police so cautious that many criminals may go undetected.

Many lawyers are also concerned about Subsection (2). Evidence obtained by threats or force has never been admissible in a trial. But a prosecutor may use evidence found as a result of such a confession. For example, if the police force a murderer to admit that he or she had committed the crime, and the murderer then leads the police to the hidden gun he or she had used, the police could use as evidence the gun and the fingerprints on it. But the confession itself could not be used against the murderer. Many lawyers believe that if the police are not able to get confessions they will demand other means to detect and convict criminals, such as wiretaps, broader search warrants, more paid informers, and so on.

As with many other sections of the Charter, the courts are given a great amount of power.

GENERAL

25. The guarantee in this Charter of certain rights and freedoms shall not be construed so as to abrogate or derogate from any aboriginal, treaty or other rights or freedoms that pertain to the aboriginal peoples of Canada including
  (a) any rights or freedoms that have been recognized by the Royal Proclamation of October 7, 1763; and
  (b) any rights or freedoms that may be acquired by the aboriginal peoples of Canada by way of land claims settlement.

---

25. The Native peoples fought hard to have a statement of their rights included in the Charter. But since no one knew exactly what these rights were, Section 25 did not define them. A later section in the constitution (35) added that "the existing aboriginal and treaty rights of the aboriginal peoples of Canada are hereby recognized and affirmed" and stated that "aboriginal peoples" included Indian, Inuit, and Metis peoples.

26. The guarantee in this Charter of certain rights and freedoms shall not be construed as denying the existence of any other rights or freedoms that exist in Canada.

27. This Charter shall be interpreted in a manner consistent with the preservation and enhancement of the multicultural heritage of Canadians.

28. Notwithstanding anything in this Charter, the rights and freedoms referred to in it are guaranteed equally to male and female persons.

29. Nothing in this Charter abrogates or derogates from any rights or privileges guaranteed by or under the Constitution of Canada in respect of denominational, separate or dissentient schools.

30. A reference in this Charter to a province or to the legislative assembly or legislature of a province shall be deemed to include a reference to the Yukon Territory and the Northwest Territories, or to the appropriate legislative authority thereof, as the case may be.

31. Nothing in this Charter extends the legislative powers of any body or authority.

26-31. These sections do not give new rights, but protect those we already have. Section 27 would permit a government to set up schools using languages of instruction other than French or English. Governments could also give grants to cultural centres. Section 28 reinforces the rights guaranteed in Section 15. However, Section 28, unlike Section 15, was not included among those that governments could avoid by the use of Section 33. In other words, this is one of the guarantees that neither Parliament nor any regislature can override. Section 31 was intended to make it clear that neither the federal nor the provincial governments had increased their powers at the expense of the other. The Charter, in fact, was simply a limitation on the power of all governments to deny Canadians their rights and freedoms.

APPLICATION OF CHARTER

32. (1) This Charter applies

(a) to the Parliament and government of Canada in respect of all matters within the authority of Parliament including all matters relating to the Yukon Territory and Northwest Territories; and

(b) to the legislature and government of each province in respect of all matters within the authority of the legislature of each province.

(2) Notwithstanding subsection (1), section 15 shall not have effect until three years after this section comes into force.

32. This section makes it clear that the Charter applies to the federal government, the provincial governments, and the governments of the Yukon and the Northwest Territories. Since local governments have only the powers given them by the provinces, the Charter would apply also to any acts, called by-laws, passed by local governments. As we have pointed out, 32 (2) gives the federal and provincial governments three years before Section 15, which guarantees equal rights for all Canadians, becomes law. This gives the governments time to review existing laws to make certain they do not conflict with Section 15.

33. (1) Parliament or the legislature of a province may expressly declare in an Act of Parliament or of the legislature, as the case may be, that the Act or a provision thereof shall operate notwithstanding a provision included in section 2 or sections 7 to 15 of this Charter.

(2) An Act or a provision of an Act in respect of which a declaration made under this section is in effect shall have such operation as it would have but for the provision of this Charter referred to in the declaration.

(3) A declaration made under subsection (1) shall cease to have effect five years after it comes into force or on such earlier date as may be specified in the declaration.

(4) Parliament or a legislature of a province may re-enact a declaration made under subsection (1).

(5) Subsection (3) applies in respect of a re-enactment made under subsection (4).

33. To many Canadians this section means that the federal and provincial governments may, in fact, deny us the rights and freedoms the Charter guarantees. The so-called "notwithstanding" provision makes it possible for a government to pass a law interfering with the sections on Fundamental Freedoms (Section 2), Legal Rights (Sections 7-14), and Equality Rights (Section 15). However, any government that intends to deny a right contained in the Charter must declare specifically that it is doing so. It must also obtain the approval of Parliament or the provincial legislature. Such a declaration would remain in effect for only five years. But it could then be passed again.

Section 33 was added to gain the agreement of the provinces to the Charter. The provinces did not want to give up the power to pass laws that did discriminate against some people in exceptional circumstances. For example, many premiers thought that the sections on legal rights would hamper law enforcement. One premier stated that it would be foolhardy to deny an elderly woman the right to refuse to rent rooms in her house to men she did not know.

Many people believed that governments would hesitate to use the "notwithstanding" clause because they would reveal publicly that they intended to deny rights contained in the Charter. However, the government of Quebec did so immediately. In Bill 62 (1982) the National Assembly put a "notwithstanding" clause in every provincial act. This meant that the Charter would not apply in Quebec. The people of Quebec would have to depend on the province's charter of human rights for protection.

The *Charter of Rights and Freedoms* is an experiment in the long history of democratic government and the rule of law in Canada. Many Canadians see it as a triumph of individual rights over the power of government. Others praise it as a great step forward in the march towards complete equality for all citizens. Prime Minister Trudeau believes that the Charter is one of his greatest accomplishments. Some Canadians, however, are not enthusiastic supporters of the Charter. They think that it is unwise to transfer power from the elected representatives of the people, who must answer to the voters at least every five years, to judges in the courts, who do not have to answer to anyone. Certainly, the success of the Charter will depend to a very large extent on the wisdom, fairness, and common sense of those men and women who sit in judgement in our courts.

THE JUDICIARY

How important are our courts? In one word — VERY! Governments make the laws. But the courts interpret and uphold them. The courts are the foundation of our legal system and the rule of law. They make up the third branch of government known as the judiciary.

If we did not believe that justice would be done in our courts, we could not believe in the existence of the rule of law. It is before a judge, or a judge and a jury, that people are found guilty or innocent. Judges decide whether the federal government or the provinces have the power to pass certain laws. They will decide whether Quebec can reject the language guarantees in the Charter, what freedom of expression means in practice, or whether we have been denied our legal rights.

Criminal and Civil Law

In general, there are two kinds of law which the courts enforce, *criminal law* and *civil law*. *Criminal law* is the same throughout all of Canada. It makes clear what is meant by such offences as murder, arson, theft, and other crimes. It also states what punishments may be set for those who are found guilty of committing such crimes. Under criminal law, all crimes are considered to be crimes against society or the community as a whole, even though they may be committed against individuals. Therefore, it is the government and not the family of a murdered person that must find the suspected criminal and bring him or her to trial in a court of law. The federal government is responsible for the criminal law.

Civil law has to do with property and civil rights. These are matters that are private to the individual citizen. Cases in civil law could involve a person's home or business or some kind of financial dealing. In civil cases, it is the individual citizen who has some kind of grievance who usually begins an action by taking his or her case to court. This is a major difference between civil and criminal cases. One exception to the general rule is traffic violations. Although traffic regulations come under civil law, violations are looked on as offences against the state. In those cases, the municipal or provincial authorities prosecute or take action against the accused.

The provincial and federal governments share authority over civil law. At first sight, this shared authority seems strange. The constitution gave the provinces control over property and civil rights, which is what the civil law is concerned with. The explanation for the "sharing" is that such matters as banking, which involve property, are controlled by the federal government. Those features of the civil law that are shared with the federal government are the same in all parts of Canada. But since the different provinces have the right to pass their own laws on property and civil rights, all other parts of the civil law may differ from province to province.

The system of civil law in Canada is also made more complicated because the province of Quebec has kept its own Civil Code, which came originally from France. In the other provinces, the laws of Britain form the basis of the civil law.

The Courts

The chart on page 186 shows the judicial system that has developed in Canada since 1867. The British North America Act gave the provinces responsibility for the administration of justice in the province and the power to establish a system of courts to enforce both criminal and civil law. It also gave the federal government power to create courts for the "better administration of justice of the laws of Canada." However, there is not a separate court system for the provinces and for the federal government. Rather, there is a single court system, shaped like a pyramid, for both civil and criminal cases. As the arrows indicate, a case usually will begin in a lower court. The decision there may be appealed to the provincial Supreme Court, and finally, to the Supreme Court of Canada. The Supreme Court of Canada is now the highest court in the country. Until 1949, some cases could be appealed from Canada's Supreme Court to the highest court in the British Empire, known as the Judicial Committee of the Privy Council. The Supreme Court of Canada not only hears appeals from the provincial Supreme Courts, it also makes the final decisions regarding federal and provincial powers. The Supreme Court will also make the final decisions on the rights and freedoms in the Canadian Charter.

The British North America Act gave the federal government the power to appoint all of the judges in the major provincial courts. Federal appointment would mean that the judges in the provincial courts would be free of any interference from the provincial government since the federal government appointed and paid them. And the fact that judges could not be dismissed easily protected them from pressure from the federal government. The consent of the House of Commons and the Senate is necessary before a Supreme Court judge can be dismissed.

All of these provisions were designed to ensure that the Canadian judiciary was completely independent of any form of political or other pressures. The independence of the judiciary is one of the foundations of the rule of law.

THE COURT SYSTEM

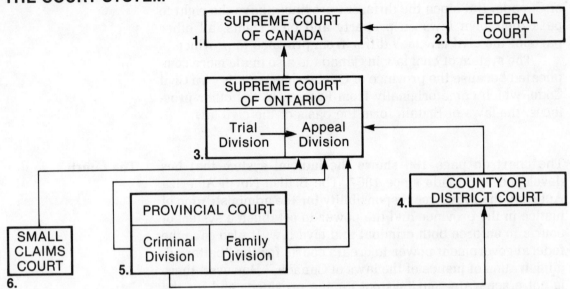

The system of courts is not exactly the same in all provinces, and the appeal procedure from the lower to the higher courts cannot be illustrated in detail. But the above chart, showing the system as it exists in Ontario, provides a general impression of the courts that handle civil and criminal cases.

1. The Supreme Court of Canada is the final court of appeal in all civil and criminal cases. However, the court may refuse to hear an appeal. It is also the court that finally decides all constitutional questions, such as those concerning the powers of the federal and provincial governments.

2. The Federal Court hears cases involving the federal government and its departments.

3. The Trials Division, known as the High Court of Justice, hears all civil cases involving more than $7500, as well as serious criminal cases. The Appeals Division hears appeals from the Trials Division and the lower courts in both civil and criminal cases. Some cases are heard by one judge, others by all eight judges.

4. County, or District, Courts hear civil cases below $7500 and also hear criminal appeals from the Provincial Court. The court can hear some criminal cases if the accused chooses trial by jury, for there are no jury trials in the Provincial Court.

All judges in the above courts are appointed by the federal government.

5. The Provincial Court, called the Magistrate's Court in some provinces, has two divisions. The Family Court hears cases concerning the family, and also cases involving juvenile offenders. Most other provinces have a separate Juvenile Court. The Criminal Division does not try the most serious criminal cases. The judges are appointed by the province. There are no jury trials.

6. Small Claims (Debts) Court hears cases involving less than $1000. In some provinces these cases are heard in the Provincial Courts. The judges are appointed by the provincial government.

The quality of our judges is also of great importance to the health of our judicial system. Of course, judges must be lawyers with some experience. The Governor General appoints judges on the recommendation of the Cabinet. In practice, the final decision is really in the hands of the prime minister and the minister of justice. There is no doubt that political considerations may have an influence on a particular appointment. For example, it is not likely that a prime minister who was opposed to increasing provincial rights would appoint a judge to the Supreme Court of Canada who was a well-known supporter of giving more power to the provinces. (It was for this reason that during the discussions about a new Canadian constitution all the provinces wanted to obtain some voice in the appointment of judges to the Supreme Court of Canada.) Nor would a prime minister who thought that the guarantee of legal rights would weaken the maintenance of law and order be likely to appoint someone who was well known as a strong supporter of those guarantees.

The Judges

More serious than making appointments with such broad political considerations in mind has been the practice of using appointments to the courts as a form of political reward.

The practice is not as common now as it once was. However, of the 25 judges on the Supreme Court of Canada and the Federal Court in 1982, three had been members of federal or provincial Cabinets. Others had been active in politics or closely linked with the party whose leader appointed them.

This is not to suggest that former politicians cannot be as independent or able as anyone else. But there may be doubts about judges so appointed, even if they are not justified. Some Canadians believe that politicians should be excluded from the Bench on the grounds that nothing should in any way lessen our confidence in the independence and high quality of those who sit in judgement in our courts.

Law in a democracy is not something that concerns only lawyers, judges, and the police. The law we live under is our law. Although we often complain about laws that we think are unfair or unreasonable, it is the law that protects our freedom, our lives, and our property. Indeed, it is the rule of law that guarantees our democratic rights and thus makes it possible for us to change the law. Cicero was right when he said, "We are all slaves of the law that we may be free." He could also have said with equal truth, "Since we are free under the rule of law we are not slaves."

STUDY GUIDE

Getting the Facts

1. Define each of the following: rule of law, libel, *habeas corpus*, abrogate, derogate, aboriginal rights, competent, by-laws, "notwithstanding" clause, political patronage, the Bench.
2. What is meant by the statement that the rule of law makes us "all slaves of the law that we may be free"?
3. What are the differences between criminal and civil law?
4. Summarize the most important rights contained in the *Charter of Rights and Freedoms*.
5. In what way is our court system similar to a pyramid?

Using the Facts

1. Is the *Charter of Rights and Freedoms* a wise document? Pierre Trudeau thinks the document is a great achievement. Other Canadians fear that the Charter gives too much power to the courts. Where do you stand?
2. Which do you value more highly, freedom or security?
3. The *Charter of Rights and Freedoms* is a very important document. It is also difficult to understand. Select the three sections you think are most important. Explain your choices.
4. Do you agree that it is important for the judiciary to be independent? Why or why not?
5. Make a speech on your rights as a Canadian, using the Charter as your only source.

Research Projects

1. Some Native people believe that the Charter does not protect their rights. What are the reasons for this point of view? What aboriginal rights do you think the Charter should contain?
2. The chart opposite shows how a criminal case proceeds from the time of arrest to the final verdict. As the chart indicates, there are two types of criminal offences. The first, Summary Conviction, includes most of the less serious offences. The second, called Indictable, includes all others. However, among the indictable offences, there are some minor ones that can be tried under procedures identical to Summary Conviction. For the more serious indictable offences, however, the procedure is more elaborate.

   Study the procedures in the cases outlined opposite. While doing so, examine the section on "Legal Rights" in the *Charter of Rights and Freedoms* and determine at what stages the Charter would protect you if you were suspected of any of the three offences. Then for one of the indictable offences, make your own chart combining the two.

CRIMINAL PROCEDURE IN ONTARIO — AN OUTLINE	CRIMINAL PROCEDURE IN ONTARIO — EXAMPLES		
	SUMMARY CONVICTION	INDICTABLE Serious	INDICTABLE Most Serious
INFORMATION An individual, usually a Police Officer, swears an information (lays a charge) under the Criminal Code.	eg. Impaired Driving (Section 234 of the Criminal Code)	eg. Break and Enter (Section 306 of the Criminal Code)	eg. First Degree Murder (Section 218 of the Criminal Code)
ARREST If arrested, the Accused is either released or appears before a Provincial Judge or Justice of the Peace. If not released, the Accused has the right to a bail hearing.	Sometimes arrested	Generally arrested	Always arrested
BAIL HEARING Depending on the charge, on the circumstances of the offence, and on the Accused's past record, bail is denied or granted. If released, the Accused is told to appear in Court at a later date.	Usually released	Sometimes released	Rarely released
APPEARANCE BEFORE A PROVINCIAL COURT JUDGE For three of the categories of offences, the Accused is subjected to a series of automatic procedures. For the fourth (see Break and Enter example), the Accused can elect (choose) a Trial Procedure.	Charge read. Accused pleads. If "Guilty," sentenced. If "Not Guilty," trial by Provincial Court Judge in Provincial Court, Criminal Div.	Charge Read. Accused chooses: (a) Trial by Provincial Court Judge (same as Summary Conviction). or (b) Trial by County Court Judge alone. or (c) Trial by County Court Judge and Jury	(See below)
(PRELIMINARY HEARING) The Preliminary Hearing is designed to determine whether there is sufficient evidence to put the Accused on trial. If there is, the Judge commits the Accused for trial; if not, the Judge dismisses the charge(s) against the Accused. The Accused is then released.	Not applicable	If (b) or (c), automatic Preliminary Hearing. If committed, Plea. If "Guilty," sentenced. If "Not Guilty," Trial.	Automatic Preliminary Hearing. If committed, Plea. If "Guilty," sentenced. If "Not Guilty," Trial.
TRIAL A trial generally consists of the following parts: 1. Charge(s) read. 2. Plea. 3. Crown evidence. 4. Defence evidence. 5. Argument by Crown and Defence. 6. Verdict. If Guilty, *Sentence*. If Not Guilty, within 30 days of sentence or acquittal, the Accused and the Crown may APPEAL (to County Court for Summary Conviction or the Supreme Court of Ontario for Indictable).	Trial before Judge in Provincial Court, Criminal Division eg. Impaired Driving For a first offence, a fine of not more than $2000 and not less than $50 (or) imprisonment for 6 months (or) both.	If (b) Trial before County Court Judge If (c) Trial before County Court Judge and Jury eg. Break and Enter If into a private residence, life imprisonment or lesser sentence. Not eligible for discharge.	Trial by Supreme Court Judge and Jury eg. First Degree Murder Imprisonment for life without eligibility for parole for 25 years.

Index

Note: *Italicized figures indicate references to illustration or caption only.*

Aberdeen, Lord, *89*
Aberhart, William, *100*
Alberta, *25*, 59, *124*, *125*, *126*, *127*, 148, 150
Amending formula, Canadian constitution, 129, 130, 140-1
Auditor General, 85

BNA Act. *See* British North America Act
Backbenchers, 77, 82
Ballot, secret, 47, 50
Bennett, R. B., *60*, 187
Bilingualism, 131-3, 137-9, 174, 176-9
    and BNA Act, 133, 139, 177
    and Canada Act, 1982, 139, 176-9
    and Official Languages Act, 137-8, 176
    and Trudeau, 136-9
Bill 101, 137-8
Bills, 75, 76-7, 78, 86
    passing a, 76-7, 78
Black, family, 107
Borden, Sir Robert 67
Britain, influence of, 14, 15, 74, 88, 185
British Columbia, *27*, 46, 59, *124*, *125*, *126*, *127*, 150
    local government in, 158-60
British North America Act, 1867, 15-17, 74, 118-20, 129, 170, 177, 185
    and bilingualism, 133, 139, 177
    and Bill 101, 137-8
    and Canada Act, 1982, 16, 177
    division of powers in, 16-17, 118-20, 123, 127, 140, 151, 184-5
    See also Federalism, decentralization of; Federal-provincial relations
Broadbent, Edward, 53, *73*
Brown, Rosemary, *52*, 53

CCF. *See* Co-operative Commonwealth Federation
CTV, 113
Cabinet, the, 17, 78-9, 81-4, 186
    and civil service, 92-3
    and collective responsibility, 82
    functions of, 14, 74, 77, 81, 84-5
    power of, 14, 81-5
    and prime minister, 65, 69, 81-2, 82-3
    and responsible government, 14, 17, 74
    selection of, 65, 81-2
    and Senate, 86
Canada Act, 1982, 15-16, 130, 139, 168-83
    amending formula for, 130, 140-1
    and *Charter of Rights and Freedoms*, 169-83
    and Quebec, 130, 140-1
Canadian Broadcasting Corporation, 108, 111-13

Canadian Daily Newspaper Publishers' Association, 107
Canadian Radio-Television and Telecommunications Commission, 106
Caucus, 77, 78, *80*
Charter of Rights and Freedoms, 139, 140-1, 168-83
    application of, 182, 185
    "notwithstanding clause," 183
    and Quebec, 139, 140-1, 183
    and Supreme Court, 184, 185
    terms of, 169-83
Chief electoral officer, 48
Civil law, 184-5
Civil liberties. *See* Legal rights
Civil service, Canadian, 91-3, 136
Clark, Joseph, 48, 53, 69, 73
Collective responsibility, cabinet, 82
Committees, parliamentary, 76, 85
Confederation, 1867, 84, 86, 118-20, 151. *See also* British North America Act
Conservative party. *See* Progressive Conservative party
Constituencies, 43, 44, 45
Constitution Act, 1867, 14, 15-16, 130. *See also* British North America Act; Canada Act
Constitution, Canadian. *See* British North America Act; Canada Act; Constitution Act
Constitution, United States, 15, 94-5
Constitutional amendment, Canadian, 129, 130, 140-1
Constitutional government, 15. *See also* Law
Co-operative Commonwealth Federation (CCF), 59. *See also* NDP
Co-operative federalism, 127-9
Courts, 184-6. *See also* Judiciary; Law
Criminal law, 184, 186
Cross, James, *134*, 135

Decision-makers, 34-5, 78, 146
Democracy, 40-53
    definition of, 12
    direct, 40
    representative, 12, 40, 43-5
    and rule of law, 166-7
    and the vote, 41-53
Democratic rights, 170
Depression, the Great, 120-3
Desmarais, Paul, *103*, 107
Diefenbaker, John, 51, 66, 67, 83
Discrimination, 43, 169, 170, 175
Division of power. *See* British North America Act; Federalism, decentralization of; Federal-provincial relations

Education, 118, 121
  bilingual, 136, 137-8
  Bill 101, 137-8
  minority language rights, 139, 178-9
  provincial responsibility, 118,
  119-20, 122, 152-3
Economy, Canadian, 24, 26-8, 120-7, 149-54
  effect on political system, 26-8, 121-7
  and equalization and stabilization policies,
  123-6
  and provincial government, 149-54
Elections, 34, 43, 45-53, 63-5
  federal, 46, 47, 48, 81
  local, 155, 161
  provincial, 41-3, 46
Environment, political, forces shaping, 22-35, 78
Executive branch of government. See Cabinet
Equalization policy, 123-5

Fairclough, Ellen, 51
Federalism, Canadian, 118-41
  decentralization of, 120-9, 141
  division of powers in, 16-17, 118-20, 123, 127,
  140, 151, 184-5
  and Quebec, 130-41
Federal-provincial relations, 118-30, 141, 148-50,
  160, 184
Federal government, definition of, 14. See also
  Federalism
Fleming, James, 111
Franchise. See Vote
Francoeur, Jacques, 103
Freedoms, fundamental, 169
Front de libération du Québec, 134-6, 173

Geography, influence on political environment,
  23, 146
Government, federal, 10-17, 22-35, 72-93
  definition and role of, 10-14
  functioning of, 72-93
  and the political environment, 22-35
  representative, 12, 40, 43-5, 46
  responsible, 13, 14, 17, 74
  See also British North America Act; Canada
  Act; Division of Power; Federalism;
    Federal-provincial relations; Government,
    municipal; Government, provincial;
    Parliament
Government, municipal, 150-61
Government, provincial, 146-61. See also
  Division of power; Federalism; Federal-
  provincial relations
Governor General, 12, 74, 76, 88-90
Gross National Product, 120, 126
Great Britain. See Britain

Health and welfare, 122-3, 150, 152
History, influence on political environment, 23,
  146
Hodges, Nancy, 51
Honderich, Beland, 103

House of Commons, 12, 74-93 passim, 170, 185
  distribution of seats in, 40, 41, 43-7
  legislative function, 74, 75-80, 86
  make-up of, 50-3
  and responsible government, 14, 17, 74
  role of mass media in, 80, 98-113 passim
  role of Opposition in, 77-9, 80
  and the Senate, 86

Immigration, 25, 26
  and Bill 101, 138-9
Irving, J. C., 107
Ittinuar, Peter, 52

Judiciary, 167, 184-7
  and Charter of Rights and Freedoms, 168,
  170-83 passim
  See also Law

Kent Commission, 104-7, 110, 111
Kent, Tom, 104
King, Mackenzie, 60, 66, 67

Language. See Bilingualism; Education
Laporte, Pierre, 134, 135
Laurier, Wilfrid, 66, 67
Law, 17, 164-87
  civil, 184-5
  court system, 185-7
  criminal, 184
  definition of, 166-7
  law-making, 75-7. See also House of Com-
  mons, legislative function
Leadership, political. See Political parties; Prime
  minister
Leader of the Opposition, 66-9, 77-9, 82
Legal rights, 135, 172-4
Legislature. See Government, provincial; House of
  Commons; Senate
Lesage, Jean, 132
Lévesque, René, 130, 132, 133, 134, 135, 137,
  138-41
Liberal party, 59, 62, 66, 68, 69
Lieutenant Governor, 118, 148
Local government, 150-61

McClung Nellie, 41, 42
MacDonald, Flora, 51, 53
Macdonald, Sir John A., 50, 66, 67, 86, 187
McDonough, Alexa, 53
McGibbon, Hon. Pauline, 148
Mackenzie, Alexander, 50
Maclean Hunter, 82, 106
Macphail, Agnes, 42
Majority, rule of, 45-7
Manitoba, 59, 125, 126, 127, 177
Marchand, Leonard, 52
Massey, Vincent, 89
Media, 30, 96-113
  and advertising, 108-10
  and government, 30, 100, 111-13

ownership of, 102-7
partisanship in, 98-102
Metropolitan government, 156-7
Metropolitan Toronto. See Toronto, Metropolitan.
Monarchy, 12, 14. See also Governor General;
    Lieutenant Governor; Queen

Native Peoples, 26, 43, 52, 175, 177, 180
Natural Resources, 26, 26, 126-7
New Brunswick, 86, 125, 126, 133, 176
New Democratic Party, 46, 52, 53, 59, 102
Newfoundland, 125, 126, 127
Newspapers. See Media; Press
Nova Scotia, 53, 62, 86, 125, 126, 127
Northwest Territories, 125, 180

October Crisis, 1970, 134-6
Official Languages Act, 137-8, 176
Old-age pensions, 123
Ontario, 28, 39, 45, 46, 65, 86, 124, 125, 151, 154,
    162
    local government in, 155-7, 158, 159, 160
Opposition, in House of Commons, 77, 78, 79, 80

Parliament, 72-93. See Cabinet; Federalism;
    House of Commons; Leader of the Opposition;
    Prime minister; Senate
Parliamentary government, 12, 14, 72-93
Parti Québecois, 130, 131, 133, 136, 139-41
Pearson, Lester B., 66, 67
Péladeau, Pierre, 102
Political parties, 33, 57-69, 146
    and elections, 45-7, 63-5
    functions of, 58-62
    leadership of, 65-9
    organization of, 62-5
    and political environment, 33
    See also individual Parties
Political system, Canadian
    definition of, 22
    influences on, 23-35, 78, 121-7, 146
Press, 30, 80, 111. See also Media
Pressure groups, 31-2
Prime minister, importance of, 40, 65-9, 74, 81-3,
    186
Prince Edward Island, 51, 86, 125, 126, 149, 151,
    160, 171
Progressive Conservative party, 46, 59, 62, 66, 69,
    162
Provincial government. See Government,
    provincial
Provincial-municipal relations, 152, 154

Quebec, 28, 62, 86, 103, 124, 125, 127, 130-41,
    185
    and October Crisis, 1970, 134-6
    and sovereignty-association, 139-41
    and Trudeau, 133, 137-9
    and Canada Act, 1982, 130, 140-1
Queen, 16, 74, 75, 88. See also Governor General;
    Lieutenant Governor

Question period, 79-80

Ralliement des Créditistes, 59
Referendum, Quebec, 1980, 103, 130, 139-41
Representative government, 12, 40, 43-5, 46
Responsible government, 13, 14, 17, 74
Ridings. See Constitutencies
Roblin, Sir Rodmond, 41
Royal Commission on Newspapers. See Kent
    Commission
Royal Commission on the Status of Women, 50
Rule of law, 17, 166-8. See also Law

St. Laurent, Louis, 66, 67
Saskatchewan, 45, 59, 124, 125, 126, 171
Schreyer, Edward, 89
Scott, Walter, 42
Senate, 14, 74, 75, 76, 85-8, 185
Shared-cost programs, 123
Sifton, family, 107
Smith, Mary Ellen, 42
Social Credit Party, 46, 59
Southam Press, 104, 107, 110
Sovereignty-association, 139-41
Stabilization policy, 125, 126
Supreme Court of Canada, 52, 127, 165, 177,
    185-7
Supreme Courts, provincial, 185, 187

Tariffs, 28
Taxes, 28, 29, 117, 126, 157
Thomson, Ken and Roy, 102, 103, 104, 106, 107
Toronto, Metropolitan, 122, 150, 155-7
Trudeau, Pierre Elliott, 40, 65, 67, 68-9, 73, 79,
    83, 183
    and Quebec, 133, 137-41

United States, 15, 26, 32, 74, 86

Values and beliefs, influence on political
    environment, 28-9
Vancouver, 158, 159
Vote, the, 40-50, 57
Votes for Women movement, 41

War Measures Act, 135
Whips, party, 78
Wilson, Bertha, 52
Women, 50, 175
    in Parliament, 42, 50-1, 53
    and the vote, 41-3

Yukon Territory, 124, 180